I0722008

Denial Kills

an anthology of

Poetry and Short Fiction

edited by

Viveca Shearin

Zack Dye

and Benjamin Gorman

Published in the United States by
Not a Pipe Publishing, Independence, Oregon.
www.NotAPipePublishing.com

Paperback Edition

ISBN-13: 978-1-948120-79-1

Cover by Benjamin Gorman

This is a work of fiction. Names, characters, places, and incidents either are products of the writer's imagination or are used fictitiously.

Table of Contents

Introduction

During the Great Depression, Roosevelt told us we have nothing to fear but fear itself. But fear isn't the only thing we, as humans, should be wary of. There is another sinister threat, something that, if not addressed before it sets in, can be deadly. Denial, when allowed to fester, can have serious consequences. For example, a woman who refuses to see the ugly truth about her doomed engagement can end up trapped in a miserable marriage. A wife who refuses to accept that her husband is unfaithful can find herself confronted by his lover, by her own jealousy, and by her own willful ignorance. Denying women the rights to their own bodily autonomy can cost us our happiness, our sanity, and our lives. Denial can take many forms. And when one isn't careful, denial can most surely kill.

Our country and our world finds itself in a very different crisis than the Great Depression. Certainly some measure of denial about the possibility of market failure contributed to that global catastrophe, and a refusal to acknowledge its severity early on muted the response that could have saved so many livelihoods. But once the deflationary cycle had set in, even the most clear-eyed observers couldn't magically undo the market collapse. Our multiple crises, in contrast, were born of a host of other vices, but it's denial which feeds them. The layered crises of a global pandemic, a racial reckoning, a spike in political partisanship, and (hopefully) the last, violent, desperate gasp of patriarchy have arisen from different sources and seem to be falling in on themselves all at once. The pandemic is the product of an unsustainable relationship to the natural world, with greed pushing humans and nature into an accelerating game of chicken we can't possibly win. Our racial reckoning is the product of centuries of oppression finally piercing into the consciousness of the dominant group who must hold onto the hierarchy or accept our role in perpetuating its evil. The spike in political partisanship is born of the lust for power, with the right in particularly accepting compromises of all their professed positions in the name of maintaining a white, male, ethno-chauvinist state. The seeming increase in misogynistic violence, like our racial reckoning, is mostly a consequence of patriarchy revealing itself as it unravels, but there is a renewed danger in the violence, both rhetorical and physical, born of the fear of the oldest oppressive system's collapse. But all of these, greed, lust, fear, and wrath, are exacerbated by a surge in conspiratorial thinking. While it may not be the cause, denial is the fuel which keeps all of these crises chugging along. We cannot solve problems we refuse to see.

The world has seen its shortcomings and insists on ignoring them. More than half a million Americans are dead because of the coronavirus, but many continue to refuse to see the disease as a real threat. We deny that slave-based economics underpins our collective understanding of labor. We deny that women have an exclusive and singular right to their own choices, to be made by themselves and their children once they are fed. We deny that our relationship to the earth could be symbiotic as opposed to parasitic. We deny that our greatest asset is the sun while we seek other planets to pollute and exploit. We deny that a sound education nurturing critical thinking allows us to collectively better explore our changing world.

Furthermore, we deny that a globalized society, moving and exchanging ideas worldwide at the speed of light, has exposed the dirtiest underpinnings of human existence. We commonly support cruelty and trauma to the young, the old, the poor, the transgendered, the non-white, the women, the disabled and the otherwise disadvantaged. As long as we deny our need to collectively heal, we repeat these cycles of death and killing.

We offer these stories in hopes of expository healing. We want a world that does not deny that its best path to healing is prevention. The more great minds we can use to solve problems, the easier we can prevent catastrophe and protect against the finality of death. After the pandemic no one can deny that we are very social beings. If we are to protect and nurture the beauty of our inherent dignity as human beings, we must accept that our babies must be fed and educated. Women, people of color and those of any identity must be protected from violence. Income cannot be based on labor but on existence itself . We must protect against the weather we've broken. We have seen what happens when the planet and its population is reduced to serving the wealthy; the world burns and floods and freezes while we watch our loved ones die.

Barack Obama, in *A Promised Land*, writes: "If we do not have the capacity to distinguish what's true from what's false, then by definition the marketplace of ideas doesn't work. And by definition our democracy doesn't work. We are entering into an epistemological crisis." It's this crisis we sought to illuminate through the poems and short fiction in this anthology. Fiction, in particular, might seem to be the wrong tool for helping to distinguish between truth and falsehood. Actually, it's the perfect tool. Like poetry, fiction makes itself known, transparently, through the form. No one reading these stories would mistake them for journalism, just as no one would look at a poem and mistake it for a piece of sculpture or a ballet or a performance of an opera. Instead, these works of art, though untrue, welcome us into the process of reckoning with truths we would rather ignore. Only six years ago, we lived in a world where politicians spun stories and massaged the truth when being completely honest would not have been politically expedient. Then we elected a president who lied to the public shamelessly over 30,000 times during his only term. And while baseless conspiracies rooted in lies and ignorance have existed for millenia, his lies led to people being separated from family members, people being targeted and singled out because of their race, ethnicity, sexual orientation, gender, and other things he refused to understand. And because of his lies, people were killed. A significant constituency of our political leaders are either too afraid to directly confront these lies, or harbor these beliefs themselves, such that they will enable, participate in, and excuse an insurrection against our nation and immediately afterwards absolve themselves and their supporters with more lies.

Witnessing this, many ask, "Where is the bottom?" But the real question we all need to be asking is, "How do we get back to a shared sense of reality?" We don't pretend to have the answer. How do we communicate anything effectively to someone who has decided reality itself is a falsehood imposed by a nefarious cabal of faceless villains? It's like trying to cross a language barrier, only with someone who has renounced language itself. We don't know how to bridge that divide. But we can shine a spotlight on the danger inherent in the refusal to accept reality. We might not ever be able to use reason to logic our way out of our epistemic crisis, but if we want to tackle the myriad of other crises we are facing simultaneously, at least those of us interested in reality can confront the awful truth that denial is deadly, and that those who embrace it have chosen to wrap their arms around their stone idols and leap into the sea. We might not be able to save them, but we can break the surface and examine our other problems in the clear air if we are willing to let them go. Denial kills. But it doesn't have to kill us all.

-Viveca Shearin, Zack Dye, and Benjamin Gorman

The Kid with the Longest Braid

by Jessica Mehta

"Beyond the cracked sidewalk, and the telephone pole with layers of flyers in a rainbow of colors, and the patch of dry brown grass, there stood a ten-foot high concrete block wall, caked with dozens of coats of paint. There was a small shrine at the foot of it, with burnt out candles and dead flowers and a few soggy teddy bears. One word of graffiti filled the wall, red letters on a gold background: Rejoice!"

The pop thundered through the classroom. Her eyes shot towards the rows of students—as always, it was an ocean of blank faces. She clutched the newspaper against her chest. "Who's got gum?" she asked. Even she could hear the fatigue in her voice. *How many times have I asked this?* She thought she saw three students swallow dramatically but couldn't be certain. Nobody. Nobody was going to confess. Two weeks in the tribal school and she was still searching for some kind of grounding. "Okay," she cleared her throat. "Now, *rejoice*. Who knows what that means?" Nothing. Endless black eyes. She tucked her hair behind her ears and pulled out the tattered dictionary from her wobbly desk. "Rejoice: Feel or show great joy or delight," she read theatrically. "Cause joy to."

"Joy?" said the kid in the back row. *What was his name?* She couldn't remember. In her mind he was The Kid with the Longest Braid. It seemed like it was taking forever to memorize names. She ran through the roster of 30 kids in her head and could see his handwriting clearly from the assignments she'd graded but couldn't come up with a name. "What they got to be joy-ful about?" he countered. "Why didn't nobody clean up those dead flowers and baby toys? Who's given dyin' things, *flowers*, to her anyway? I mean, she got killed three years ago—"

"Enough," she said as she smacked the newspaper onto the desk. "It's the anniversary of her ... death ... and that's not what we're supposed to be discussing with this article anyway. The purpose, if you recall, is to compare how an op-ed piece is different than—"

"I heard she got flattened so fast her shoes came clean off," Irma piped up from somewhere in the back. She wriggled in her seat with dark eyes darting around the room, ready for a fight.

Before she could reply, diffuse the situation, The Kid with the Longest Braid whirled around in his seat. "Imma whoop your ass—"

"Stop," she said as firmly as she could. It took everything in her not to slouch down into the cracked vinyl seat and rest her head on the desk like over half the students had been doing all day. "It doesn't matter ... that's not what we're talking ... nevermind. Now, I made everyone photocopies of this opinion piece." *With my own money,* she thought with a touch of bitterness she'd never known in herself until she'd arrived here. *Snap out of it. You're the one who wanted this.* "As we discussed earlier, we're going to spend the Quiet Hour writing our response to the article. If you have any questions on the details, refer to the board. Again, it's between 250 and 300 words regardless of how big you write or how many pages you fill. And handwriting *will* count for part of your grade, so don't try writing excessively large. That's the first trick they teach teachers." She offered a smile at the class, a lightening with a joke, but nobody responded. "Now, you'll be writing a personal response to this op-ed article so it can be anything you like. Remember, this is for your creative writing credit so there's some wiggle room, but please do pay attention to the grammar we've been studying. Remember, a passive voice—"

"I won't do it," The Kid with the Longest Braid said simply. For emphasis, he shoved his notebook as far across the little desk as possible and crossed his thin arms over his chest.

She sighed. "I don't have time for this. What do you mean you're not going to do it? Everyone, pencils out. You have five minutes to re-read the article *quietly* to yourselves before we start. If you want to use the pencil sharpener, it's one at a time, one row at a time." She could have given the spiel half-asleep and it wasn't even October yet. She still caught some jostling of students to get out of their seats first in the front row from the corner of her eye.

"What, you don't hear too good? I said I'm not gonna do it." The Kid wasn't budging, and his pencil remained unmoved on his desk. She sized him up. Just ten years old, but with a knowing in his eyes of a man. For the first time in her teaching career, a fifth grader scared her. Ms.Washington pulled herself up to her full height, activated her axial length like they were always talking about in yoga class, and took a shaky breath.

"You either open that notebook right now or you're going to the principal's office." He didn't break their eye contact, still as the moment between hunter and prey. *Please open the goddamned notebook,* she willed. The principal's office was an empty threat, and she wasn't sure if the kids knew that. The principal was never there. And when she was, the last thing she had time for was babysitting a moody student.

"So do it. I don't care," The Kid said. He eased back in his seat and eyed her.

She realized she'd been holding that deep breath and her lungs began to ache. It came out in a rush. "*Shit,* now look here—"

"Ooohh!" the kids said en masse as the forbidden four-letter word slipped out of her mouth. "Ms. Washington said a bad word! She—"

"*Enough,*" she shouted to the class. Immediately silence settled over everyone. It was the first time she'd ever raised her voice in the classroom. The first time she'd raised her voice in any classroom. "Get up, you're coming with me." She took a step towards The Kid and prayed that he'd get up. Get up. *Get up.* All those hours of being told over and over how you *never* put a hand on a student, all the horror stories of the consequences, flooded through her. Did those rules apply at a tribal school? On Indian land? She didn't know. She knew they had their own police department, laws, everything. *Can I lift him by the elbow without going to jail?*

Surprisingly, he got up easily as she approached, but there was something different about him. His shoulders didn't slouch forward like usual and his eyes still held hers, tight, almost like a lover. Ms. Washington had never had a real conversation, one on one, with him but that wasn't that unusual. His dad had shown up for the one parent-teacher conference to start the year, but as per the school's requirements the students stayed home. *Wait, the dad had shown up, right? This kid was the one whose mother wasn't there, wasn't he?* Now she couldn't remember. He faced her coolly. All she could read in him was opaque. "Forget the principal's office," she hissed. "I'm not about to bother her with this." She grabbed his notebook, copy of the article, and chewed-up pencil. Side by side, they began to march towards the back of the room like well-trained soldiers. "You'll go sit in the cubby room and write this fu—freaking paper if it takes you all day."

He stopped so quickly she was two strides ahead of

him before she realized. "And what if I don't?"

Ms. Washington turned slowly. The tension in the room was palpable. She could feel dozens of eyes on the two of them, little faces hungry for drama to gossip about during break. "You will. Or you'll stay there until you do."

"You think that scares me? You think keepin' me here is a threat? You have no idea, do you?"

Before she could think, before she could doubt herself, she reached towards him and grabbed his arm. It wasn't until she'd hurled him into the huge cubby closet where jackets and sack lunches were stored that she realized he was still a child. His weight in her grip shocked her. It was like releasing a bird.

"Just get in there," she said as she pressed his materials firmly against his chest. She shut the heavy wooden door slowly, each creak of the rusted hinges begging her to slam it. Somehow she resisted. "What are you staring at?" she asked the class without looking at any of them. "Get to work."

  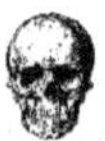

When the final bell of the day rang, she let the students rush to the cubby closet and release him. Ms. Washington tried not to look, not to see, and kept her head bowed over her desk as she pretended to grade papers. There was chattering and the rustling of jackets to help drown out her thoughts. They filed out in a mad group, caught only by her peripherals. She didn't know if The Kid was among the first or last to power walk out of the classroom and into the dusty autumn afternoon.

What she did know is that throughout the rest of the day following The Incident, four long hours, there were no sounds from the cubby room. Not once did he emerge with a shy hand up motioning towards the bathroom. At recess, she stared at that proudly shut door and almost, *almost,* got up to check on him. But she didn't. The volunteer recess staff filed her class in and out for their fifteen minutes on the dried-up grass and didn't even notice that one was missing. *Thank God this all happened after lunch,* she thought. Ms. Washington didn't know if it was pride, anger, or some kind of feral-ness inside her but she wasn't certain she would have been able to let him out even to eat.

When she was sure all the students were gone, and the scuffs and squeaks on the linoleum in the hallway faded to silence, she stood up. It was the longest walk across her classroom she'd ever taken, longer even than her very first day at this foreign school that seemed a throwback to a time she hadn't lived. The cubby room door had been left slung open, and she could see the long-forgotten moth-eaten hoodie hanging from a plastic hanger. It had been there since the start of the school year two weeks ago, and likely for years before that. Part of her thought she'd still see him in there, stubborn and ready to fight. But there was nobody. Sitting squarely on the low empty shelf where students put their snow boots in the winter was his notebook. The copy of the article was gone.

Ms. Washington sat down on the dirty shelf, not

caring that the dust and grime would stain her yellow pencil skirt. She opened the notebook to nothing. Nothing. Page after page of nothing. "Damn," she said under her breath. As she flipped towards the center, the crisp empty pages gave way to drawings. Profiles of a middle-aged woman crafted with such skill and detail she briefly wondered if someone else had done it—an adult, someone with years of training. But something in her marrow told her this was all him. The profiles of the woman gave way to incredibly detailed sketchings of a little girl with twin braids. She looked mildly familiar, but then again there was a preschool connected to the tribal school and it could easily be one of the many toddlers she nearly tripped over every day getting to the classroom. He'd filled dozens of pages with intricate portraits of the little girl, occasionally punctuated with images of the woman. With each flip of the page, the girl's braids became stronger. Thicker. Somehow writhing on the page with such severity the pages nearly rattled in her hands. The woman's braids grew heavier, too, dangerous, ready to strike. She couldn't tell how old the sketches were, but it must have taken him weeks, months, if not years to complete this kind of expansive portfolio. She let out a sigh as she slowly flipped towards the end of the notebook. Just as she was about to close it, just as her heart softened for him, she turned to the last page. It was filled with his neat handwriting, a slanted cursive that leaned so heavily to the right the words looked close to toppling over.

Rejoyse? Re-joy? There wasn't no joy in the 1st place All *these jornalis actin like Mimis death spot is some kind of memoryal is stupid They dumb or somthing???? Dont they get taut better than that in collage??? The stupid ass holes who rote that on Mimis spot dont no anything about nothing + she HATED teddybears She said they were scary and thot theyd come alive at nigt Dont the jornalis now that??? and all thos flowers are dum to Why are peple leving stuff thats gonna die that dosnt make sense If they realy want to give stuff to Mimi they shuld give stuff she like d like huming bird eyrings or choklit Evry one is talking abot the wall and all the ~~pant~~ PAINT like its som kinda secret and thats dum to I can tell no NDN rote this OPPED thing or whatevr EVRYONE nos why Mimi colord that wall difrent colors You all stupid???? Thats ~~her~~ Wher R mama was killd + now Mimi killd ther to and mama got raypt + left ther + all thos peple riting badshit abot mama mayd Mimi mad I was mad to but Mimi brav E enuff to do somthing Mimi p a int over all the bad stuff evry time No body gonna call mama a hor or slut + If id ben with Mimi that day I dont think she wud got killd cuz with 2 of us that car wud saw us She was to litle but lots bravr then me But im gonna do what i shudda don b4 im gonna make it rite i dont no how many words this is but thats all THE END*

"My God," she whispered as she let the notebook fall shut in her lap. She stood and took deliberate steps back to her desk, heels clicking like gunfire. She pulled out the bright violet stack of Post-It notes, brand-new and bought from her own funds at the start of the year. *A,* she wrote boldly with her new bronze Sharpie pen. When she'd started teaching, she swore she'd never use red. It was too aggressive and nobody wanted to try to resuscitate a dying paper. Black was just too somber. Now, she wished for somber. For something suitable for a funeral. Looking at the naked "A", she added a plus sign. *Come talk to me,* she added. It wasn't enough and reeked of an afterthought, but it was all she had. She placed the notebook on The Kid's desk, stood back, then straightened it so it was aligned perfectly in the center.

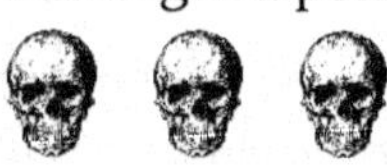

It took her two hours to get ready the next morning, ninety minutes of which involved simply pulling herself out of bed. There was a dread settled in her throat heavy as an autumn nesting bird. She came up with scores of excuses not to go into the classroom. It's not like it would be an anomaly at the school anyway. They'd jumped at the chance to hire her, even though the only indigenous blood she could claim was a grandfather who said he had some kind of Cherokee in him, and even she knew everyone said that. But she had a teaching degree from one of the Ivy League schools most people forgot about and the kind of youthful energy school administrators thought could handle these kids. As she slipped into the cool seat of her little coupe, something else took the wheel. She didn't know how or why, but instead of her usual route along smooth paved roads, she took the side streets that snaked towards that fall-apart memorial. She rounded the corner and saw a gathering of people, all ages, from babies cradled on those decorative boards everyone seemed to have to elders with their hand-carved canes. They looked like disciples, tired and weary at the end of their pilgrimage. Disciples or a riot in the making.

She couldn't make out where they were all coming from. In seconds it had grown from a dozen people to twenty. Thirty. She was surrounded. Ms. Washington slowed to a crawl as she approached, forced into stillness by the mob. *This isn't normal. Is it?* she wondered. The crowd shifted slightly and she could make out a milk crate at the base of the painted wall, right in the center. The Kid was unmistakable, his braid oiled and shining in the morning light. He carried a bullhorn in his hand, held together with duct tape. But him draped in regalia, the bullhorn became Excalibur. Her car came to a stop, engulfed by people who easily stepped around the freshly waxed vehicle. She pulled up the emergency brake and stepped into the midst. Arms folded in like wings, she wove her way through the crowd toward him.

The Kid got up onto a milk crate and raised his hand. A murmur went through the crowd and then it fell silent, except for a few people shouting words of encouragement at him. The Kid acknowledged them with a nod and a shadow of a smile. In the full light of day, he looked less angry. Nearly beautiful. He waited until people stopped shouting. A siren could be heard, maybe five or ten blocks away. The Kid raised the bullhorn, pressed the button, and began to speak.

His heart battered at his chest and though it felt like his hands were shaking, when he looked down they were still. *Myocardium,* he thought to himself. *Be quiet.* In the brigade of faces, some were familiar, but he couldn't think of names. Either his father hadn't heard about the rally, which was doubtful given how fast words spread, or he'd chosen not to come. It didn't matter either way. As he lifted the bullhorn to his lips, there were no words prepared. He simply trusted that what needed to be said would come.

"My mama was killed here five years ago," he said. Silence washed across the crowd. Never before had he held such command. It fueled him, and for once he felt heard. "My sister, Mimi, two years later. I ..." He felt tears begin to sting in his eyes. *Shit, I thought I was over all this.* He glanced down and was taken by a pair of clear blue eyes, alien in the crowd. Ms. Washington gazed up at him, the only white person in a sea of familiar. At the sight of her, even with the anger from yesterday rinsed out of those bright eyes, he felt a rage start to build in his center. It overrode the sadness. "I didn't wanna believe it. When they told me," he said. "And they never caught the guy that, you know, with my mama. But that don't mean anything because I know. We all know," he continued. "It doesn't matter a *damn* who it was. Because this is what I know for sure: It wasn't any of us. Mama, she was working in the city the night she never came home. She was *dumped* here, police know that."

As if on cue, the sirens finally arrived. He saw the rez police trucks sidle up to the outskirts of the crowd. Faces he'd known his whole life in their tan baseball caps and shiny badges began to approach. One mumbled something incoherent into his walkie talkie. "Go on, son," one of the elders urged.

"We know this—my mama wasn't raped on this land. Wasn't murdered here either, at least it didn't start here. My guess, it was a setup. A *sloppy* setup. Come dump her body on the rez and nobody'd look nowhere because the secrets kept here aren't like nothing else."

"Get down," one of the officers yelled gruffly from the sidelines. "Or we'll help ya with it."

"Leave him alone, that little boy—" Ms. Washington rushed at the police, but he just tipped his head back and laughed. The Kid watched as she faltered, uncertain.

"I don't need no white savior," The Kid spoke clearly into the bullhorn. "Especially not you."

"And she don't have any power to be saving anybody anyhow," the officer added. "Now, get down, boy. You're riling everyone up."

"That's the point," he said firmly. "Don't—don't you think we should be riled up? I'm telling you, my mama was dumped here. My sister ran over in a hit and run by a coupla drunks, and all because *someone* or some people were writing that shit on this, I don't know, this some kinda grave. *Shouldn't we be "riled up?"*

"Kid's got a point," the elder said with a slow nod. "Wasn't like this before. And that trash that kept getting' written here—"

"Investigation's ongoing," the cop said with a shrug.

"We're not inviting any kind of vigilante justice here. Why don't all you folks go on home, and *you*," he said pointedly to the boy. "Shouldn't you be in school?"

The boy choked down a laugh. "School? This is crazy ..."

The walkie talkie rambled something that couldn't be made out. "C'mon then, boy," the cop said as he pushed through the crowd. "You're comin' with me."

"No," he said. He pressed the bullhorn closer to his lips. "And there's nothing you can do about it. I'm not doing anything wrong. None of us here are doing anything wrong. You're the one s'posed to fix this. When are you gonna fix all this? This is *your* job—"

"Don't think I won't beat your ass like your daddy shoulda." The cop leaned closer, nearly nose to nose thanks to the quivering milk crate beneath the boy's feet. "Maybe if there'd been more discipline at home, your mama and little sister of yours would still be alive."

The boy felt the bullhorn drop from his fingers but never heard it hit the ground. A cool licking began at his elbows. Even through the buckskin, he could feel the rhythm. The crowd merged into one, a living, breathing single entity. "Oh, my God," he heard a voice say. Ms. Washington's. He didn't know where the cop's face went or why he was suddenly somehow facing the wall. The letters were so big, so vibrant, that all he saw was red. REJOICE was gone, or maybe he was inside it. He didn't know, all he knew is that there was a fire within him that burned something fierce yet wrapped him in comfort. It felt like his mama's arms, the squeeze of his sister's small hand, his grandmother's paper-thin hands on his cheeks.

"... the hell is that ..." a voice broke through his basking, but just barely. The question poked at the perimeter of his being, an annoyance he easily pushed away. He was weightless. *Ecdysis.* There was no more creaking milk crate beneath his feet, but somehow he was solid. He was held.

"Snake," he heard a voice shout somewhere in the distance. It was far away, stretches away. The voice was afraid, but he wasn't, even as he felt the slithering make its way from the small of his back up his spine and stretch across his shoulder blades. Wings that had been waiting to be birthed.

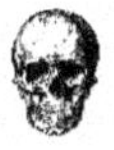

Nobody talked about it, that was the strangest part. Ms. Washington could pack everything she'd brought into the classroom in just two canvas totes. It wasn't in the local news, and it seemed nobody off the reservation had been there—besides her. But when she gave her notice to the principal, the big-bellied woman just shrugged and pushed the termination paperwork towards her.

"You, I mean ... the school has substitutes, right?" The principal just shrugged again, and Ms. Washington couldn't tell if it was a positive or negative gesture. "I ... I don't want you to think, like, it's because, you know ..."

"Because what? You got a better offer?" The principal barely looked at her, skimmed across the young teacher's face like she was no more real than a ghost.

"What? No!" Ms. Washington said. "What I meant was—"

"Want an apple?" the principal asked, pushing a woven basket of Red Delicious toward her. "My granddaughter just picked them this weekend."

"Uh—I was saying—"

"Ms. ... Washington, was it?" The principal glanced at the paperwork as if she didn't know her name. She let out a short rumble of a laugh as she bit into the gleaming red skin. "You think we haven't seen this before?" she asked as she chewed. "You know how many Michelle Pfeiffers we get out here wanting to play *Dangerous Minds*? Honestly? You lasted longer than I thought you would. Damn, now I owe the librarian five dollars. Don't you worry about it," she said. "You can tell yourself you did real good. Look at you! Went and saved yourself some Indian babies and it only took you a week."

"*Two!* And anyway, that's not what I meant. And," she straightened up in the chair with its unforgiving slats like a skeleton. "And *furthermore,* I don't think you're allowed to talk to—"

"*Lady.* Ms. *Washington.*" She put down the apple and wiped a handkerchief across her lips. "You know what we're dealing with here? You think it matters at *all* if these kids can spell 'cat?' We've got 84 percent of our women dealing with violence in their lifetime. *Eighty-four.* We've got 30 percent of our kids in poverty. We've got god knows how many people raping and assaulting our women and 96 percent of 'em *aren't Native.*" She leaned forward. "You think your little math quiz is gonna solve that? You think you can do a *damn* thing about any of that?"

Ms. Washington opened her mouth. *Say something, anything.* Nothing. She choked on the absence, couldn't close her jaw. It gaped open, unhinged, hungry and waiting.

"That's what I thought," the principal said. She held Ms. Washington's eyes a breath longer than necessary. "Go on, then," she said, softer. "Shit. You never even had a chance."

Ms. Washington's mother had sighed deeply when she'd called her to say she was leaving. "Didn't I tell you?" she asked. "You're better than that, running off to 'do good' at some poor school with those *In*—well, you know. You're an *Ivy League college-educated woman*. What were you thinking?"

"I don't ... I'm sorry," she'd muttered into the phone. "You're right." What was she supposed to say? That one of her students' braids had turned into a snake and he'd glided towards the heavens?

There was no way she was going to stay, not after what had happened. When The Kid's braid began to hiss and S-curve up his back, she'd stumbled backward, nearly fell. The cop was the only one who followed suit, bulleting through the crowd to his cruiser. The others pushed closer while still keeping a respectable distance.

It's like they'd seen it before, and maybe they had. And she could have sworn The Kid's feet weren't touching the crate. He was floating, eyes closed and face cast upward.

She had wondered at who shrieked "Snake!" so close to hear it almost burst her eardrum until the young woman gently brushed her forearm. "That's not a snake like you think," the woman said quietly, a closed-lipped smile pressed across her face. Then she said another name, one with ancient roots that wouldn't fit in Ms. Washington's mouth. "You know what this is, don't you?" the woman asked her without taking her eyes of The Kid. "This is a blessin'. You're witnessing a blessing from the ancestors. From Creator."

Ms. Washington had barreled back to her car, not daring to look back. The Kid had drawn everyone so close that there were no more human obstacles to weave her little coupe around. For a moment she thought the engine wouldn't start, just like in a horror movie, because what else could this be? But it hummed to life with ease. As she'd pulled away, she risked one look into her rearview mirror. *Am I imagining all of this?* The crowd had fallen crack-boned to their knees. The Kid floated, there was no denying it, his head nearly reaching the top of that high painted wall. So high that REJOICE lay like a promise at his feet.

A note on the story: The number of murdered and missing indigenous women (MMIW) in the US and Canada has reached epidemic proportions. While there is no comprehensive data in the US, as an example: indigenous people make up two percent of all people in Washington state but five percent of missing persons. The majority are women and girls. While The Kid with the Longest Braid *is obviously a work of fiction, it addresses very real issues and utilizes a wide range of symbolisms that pay homage to this systemic trend of violence and oppression within indigenous communities. For instance, the only named characters are female and Mama, Mimi, Irma and [Ms.] Washington, an acronym for MMIW; the symbolism of snakes within many Native tribes represent re-birth; hummingbirds are often considered healers and symbolize love and joy in many Native American cultures; and "apple"—particularly Red Delicious—is both native to Washington and a derogatory term for Native Americans.*

Speaking in Tongues

by Lydia K. Valentine

*Dedicated to the families of Trayvon Martin, Michael Brown,
Tamir Rice, and too many others to name.*

When they come
    in this time-
    in this place-
Niemoller's Socialists are not first.

The strange flotsam jettisoned
with guns, garbage bag nooses,
metal-lined vans, and more guns
are named

Amadou,
and Oscar,
Trayvon,
and Michael,
Sandra,
and Tamir

to #SAYTHENAME of a few.

In this time-
    In this place-

Our rage-full voices spill out in protest, but
the dam you fashion from concrete blocks of

DenialDetractionDisbeliefDisinterst
DenialDetractionDisbeliefDisinterst
DenialDetractionDisbeliefDisinterst
DenialDetractionDisbeliefDisinterst
DenialDetractionDisbeliefDisinterst
DenialDetractionDisbeliefDisinterst
DenialDetractionDisbeliefDisinterst
DenialDetractionDisbeliefDisinterst
DenialDetractionDisbeliefDisinterst
DenialDetractionDisbeliefDisinterst
DenialDetractionDisbeliefDisinterst

stops the viscous swamp of our agony
from reaching you.

While you watch from the banks of privilege,
we wade in water as thick and ropy as clotted dreams:
to live while black...
to marry who we love...
to use the bathroom in peace...
to keep pipelines out of ancestral lands...
to escape land mines, genocide, and other thieves
that steal our children and grandmothers.

Denial Kills

We wade in the water trying to have the breath to live,
the peace to live, the un-endangered-ness to - simply -
live.

Our light bright to midnight skin warps and prunes.
The water stirs and pulses with our voices,
our steps, and pushes against your concrete impassivity.

You look away and began to consider-
blustery defensiveness stops any progress,
but you *begin* to *consider* the sandbags
you've stacked and keep on hand to
– righteously! – protect your position.

But now,

in this time-
in this place-

Now the shore deteriorates beneath you,
you who had stood so certain, so safe before.

Now you reach out your hand, hoping
to share in our buoyant resilience.

Now you speak out in confusion and fear,
beginning to imagine the torment
of drowning by degrees in the sputum
of ruptured justice and democracy.

You.

You remind- no, scold! – us
that *movements are stronger*
when we come together
even though the barrier between
us was built by your hands,

and we are asked– no, admonished! -
to disregard that dam and the damning
consequences of your past silence,
even though the raw-meat smell
of our children's blood clings to both.

Forgive and forget slithers smoothly
from transgressors' tongues. You present
these nonsense syllables as if you're an
oracle of the divine, but your purpose,
your ploy, is far from holy. I know.

Still, I will raise my hand from the
chest-deep depths I have come to know.
I will reach across the rough concrete
of your ignorance and help you stand
in your new waterlogged reality,
in your pool that barely reaches the knee.

I dare you to call yourself a survivor.

Performance Anxiety

by Kaia Valentine

My lover cracks an egg over her head. She laughs, gripping her stomach so her innards don't fall out. She oozes love for me; it drips out of her eyes and stains her clothes. She heats our breakfast, leftovers, on the air hockey table. She molests the DJ, asking him to play our song. And every hour on the hour, that young DJ plays Hotel California. We dance in wide, oblong circles, slippery on skates we rented decades ago. We split our sides to never-ending melancholy. She's named for flowers, but she cannot bear to go outside. It's not safe for our better half, for women, fearsome roses with castrated thorns. I cannot keep her safe where wild men gnash their teeth, their yellow eyes on her breasts. Young lovers come to skate, then leave, matriculate to engagements, mortgages, flocks of fat babies fill their warm homes. We skate, untethered, in our gum-stuck, neon, game.

The lips she loaned me were once given to a rich boy, a dull, handsome boy, beneath a ripe plum tree. He wore a white t-shirt and vintage, light blue Levi's. He spoke honest, pleasant nothings. His smile was a lake without any wakes or ripples. They walked hand in hand for years without a glance. He asked her once, just after making love in his red Chevy truck-bed if she'd summer with his family. St. Moritz with a nice boy, a gentle boy, her satin toes amongst the wealthy, white sand beaches, a cosmopolitan lifestyle, her cocktails paid for. She left this at the altar. The tall boy, the easy, educated, uncomplicated, boy without an ounce of trauma, works in leveraged finance with his Father, God, on Wall Street. I bought my lover a Frito slushie (coke, cherry, and blue raspberry were out), and she bought ten more tokens for my favorite game.

My lover wears a ring on her pinkie finger as if we could marry. She cut off the others because we're monogamous. Her hand still bleeds sometimes. I asked her once, just after college, to be mine forever. The fool, bless her heart, agreed. She sings stupid songs about our love revolving around her last finger. She caresses me, massages my worn muscles. I get shin splints from our daily dances. Every hour on the hour, in the rink, she asks if I remember how we fell in love. I lie and tell her I don't. I love when she tells it. She tells frequent, pastel, white lies written in pink, bubblegum, idyllic chalk. She says,

"Once, there was a princess. She wore prince's clothes. Her bank account was a pauper's. Her parents were Mother Goose and Old King Cole. She never met them, but she had their pictures. She sold stories on street corners for hot meals. She was an honorary student at the college for well-rounded, liberal, quite affluent, youth. The nobles loved her; her apparent poverty made them feel generous. She was quick-witted, utilitarian, black, high on weed, larger than life. She wrote a story for me, totally free of charge. In her story, I marry the sweet boy, the enamored boy, happily by the plum tree. She plays lyre music at the wedding reception. Then she rudely asks the bride to bum a smoke. She wears clown makeup. When I ask her why, she says, 'It's rude to be barefaced at weddings.' I told her her story's stupid. We fell hard in love. I followed her from the place whence we fell to over by the claw machine, where I will die in love, in her arms."

Before she met me, she summered in Martha's Vineyard, cruised cool, Alaskan waters, held sea turtles in her delicate, beautiful, talented hands. She's gone ziplining, put locks on Paris bridges, Hong Kong, Amsterdam with her boarding school. Now, she holds her breath 'til her face turns dazzling purple. She makes a balloon animal out of my tongue. She crosses her legs, watching as I destroy Pacman. She wanted children. I can't give her any. Yesterday, I bought her fries that I cannot afford. She ate them, thanking me for everything I am. She washed my feet and gave a lightly dusted pedicure with clear polish, which I ruined when we donned our skates to dance. 'Cus every hour on the hour, Sebastian, the young, weathered DJ, who desperately hates us, plays our song.

In Street Fighter, I play as Ken Masters. In Mortal Kombat, I'm Subzero, unless Scorpion calls. *"Get over here,"* I demand. She, my lover, watches as I rank higher and higher. She buys our marijuana. The rink's owner, Willy, lets us smoke inside 'cus he feels sorry for me. Willy has a wife and kids, three kids. He has three family portraits on his scattered desk. I pay our rent in Blow-Pops I've bought with tickets. He counts the flavors on his desk at each month's end. He moans my name. He needs much more from me. After all, he has a family to support.

"My wife don't put out no more, and I'm so lonely. I'm so very lonely..." Willy sings the National Anthem to me, as a stark reminder. He feels sorry for the gash between my legs, but doesn't say so because sex, religion, politics, and female genitalia are strictly forbidden, foreign topics in the rink.

We share a bed with Zoltar in his fortune box. I ask him, *"Would you vouch for your soul to your God?"* He says, *"If you do not mind, friend, it doesn't matter."*

Easy for a plastic man to say— he has a penis *(or the implication thereof)*. My achievements are measured by mounting debt, a driver's license inscribed 'female', and a flawless deadshot on Terminator 2. My blue-eyed baby, soft as powdered snow, gets my six with the red gun.

A thousand heterosexual couples pass us, dreadfully all the same. The woman, long-haired, starry-eyed, impressionable, says, *"My love, my honor, win me a prize from this wonderful machine."*

The man, broad-shouldered, passive, the opportunist, says, *"Those machines are rigged! Nobody ever wins them."*

Then she pouts, they leave, they make love without any care for their good fortune. I win every time I play. The trick is to line up the claw with your dwindling expectations and then close your eyes before

you press the button. God is always watching. The machine loves me. I won my love two distinct, rare, incredible prizes: a stuffed stork and a plum black, pretty boy-child. He's bad at arcade games, outside he's a target, and he's not mine.

She wanted children. She's white with red hair. She wanted three girls. Three good girls with long legs, foul mouths, and terrible manners. Instead, Willy asked her to sit on his lap while I was looking at him. He was slurring his words, drunk on power. He's our landlord and the rink's rules are his Bible. They're unspoken, implied, dirtier than his unserviced bathrooms. If we want to stay, my love sits on his lap. I tell her not to, but she writes a poem about powerlessness. It's called "We Cannot Afford Eviction." Anyway, she reminds me, she always wanted children. I cannot provide.

Willy's a rough man, a cowardly, ugly man, a luckless man. He stinks of boredom and unwashed, wasted potential. He has shaggy hair that he cakes with disgusting grease. He barks at Sebastian when he plays anything but classical music. He's pretentious. He does not know how to read. He has four children. He has three at home. His plump, sweet fourth is mine. I write him bedtime stories out of mashed up video game instructions. I milk the token machine to fill his bottle. I steal straws and napkins to build his bassinet. I love him, almost. He is what I always wanted split in two.

I wanted children too. I wanted tender-headed, sloppy, brainy, cuties with compassionate smiles. I wanted them to have my grandma's grit, my grandpa's charm, my father's wit, and my mother's radical courage. I got a happy, impressive, disciplined boy with hair that curls into his giant, perfect ears and Willy's beady, bloodshot eyes. She told me she was pregnant. I voted abortion. She insisted she'd have one. She drew pretty pictures of our life post-pregnancy. She promised she'd manage to wriggle us free. She smiled bright, and we sang Hotel California. I thought we were fine. My lover whistled Dixie.

I wanted to come to her appointment. She said it was in Candy Land, and she was worried that I couldn't walk that far in my tattered Adidas. She said she'd be fine. She said she'd play Hotel California on the way there and giggle about me the entire way back. She said the lobby would probably smell like bleach, which makes me gag. She said she'd read somewhere it's easier alone.

She shuffled out the door a week before the morning sickness started. At first, I thought it was a grim side effect of surgery. She turned green. Her breasts were always too tender to touch. She said the smell of rental skates sickened her. Fatigue prevented our dances. She only wanted nachos and fries. She couldn't poop. She couldn't stop peeing. I started getting suspicious by the second week of symptoms. She confessed that she did not have the abortion. She said he was the only thing I couldn't give her.

It was on that point that I hyper-fixated. I became the broken arcade machines tucked into the back corner. With an 'Out of Order' sign across me, men walked by without a second glance. I'm no threat to them. There are no challenges here. High scores deleted. Those men, listless, lucky, looking for a score, could come inside my lover's batting cage, hit one good ball dead on, and do the one thing that I'd kill them all to do: give her a baby. They would frighten, block her number, leave the state, change their names promptly, or perhaps, ask to co-parent. I would love that child to death.

Instead, I rock Willy's child gently 'til he falls asleep at night. His honey breath is a tender betrayal. His diaper bag weighs on my suicidal thoughts. His coos remind me of my inadequacies. I cannot get it up, the broken machine's lifeless, flaccid joystick. We stop making love. I try, but I always think of Willy's nauseating face, her body on his abusive, undeserving lap, Zoltar's plastic dick, and the strap-on in my glowing red, insert coin pocket. I try, but I think of wealthy, studly boys with good financial careers. I think of shooting blanks inside her and the ripe plum trees swinging between blessed legs. My beautiful baby boy breaks my joystick clean off. He laughs, and Willy screams at him for breaking merchandise. He looks just like him. Sebastian drowns his screams out with Hotel California. My lover dances, softly, to neon nostalgia, which reminds us to pretend that we were ever free.

Yes, Dear, Cancer Can Kill a Trans Woman

by Claudine Griggs

It was almost two years ago that Alexandria called me with the news. A routine mammogram had turned up a suspicious area on her right breast, and further screening would be necessary. As you might expect, Alex was concerned, and her voice quavered slightly when she said, "The doctor told me not to worry because 9 out of 10 times these things turn out to be a benign cyst, but they want to do a diagnostic mammo...with an ultrasound if needed. I'm going on Friday for the follow-up."

I told her I'd take off to accompany her, but she responded, "Don't worry about it. I'm happy to go alone, and there's no need for both of us to miss work. Besides, the doc said it's probably nothing, so let's assume that's true."

Alexandria is a male-to-female transsexual, and in childhood she was brought up to be tough, to hide emotions, to pretend that a broken bone or concussion was simply an inconvenience to be dealt with after finishing your day's business. Her dad is still a military officer and advocate for a creed that few people can live by—nor should they in my opinion. But when growing up, Alexandria (Alexander until she was 22) tried to be as macho as her father. She didn't succeed, obviously, and became herself soon after graduation from college. Thank God, too, because for me, Alex is the stuff dreams are made of. Before we met, I had dated many women, but I loved Alex from the first time we met in law school. She was smart, witty, and beautiful and had a stout Lauren Bacall-ish voice. She dropped out of legal studies during our second semester and switched to a graduate program in English, finally becoming a professor at Rhode Island College. Law would never have suited her, but she had still been trying to make her dad proud and thought being a lawyer might do it. She's much happier as a teacher than she would ever have been as a legal practitioner, and frankly, I doubt anything could make her military father proud of his trans daughter. He doesn't care much for me either.

So when Alex told me that she'd go alone for the follow-up medicals, I put my foot down. "Forget it, Babe. I'm coming. That's what husbands do—even ambulance chasers like me." She smiled at my playful self-deprecation, but I sensed that Alex was relieved I would be with her even though she tried not to show it.

We went to South County Hospital that Friday. They did the extra mammogram and then whisked us to the ultrasound room; the doctor scanned and then hemmed and hawed for several minutes and said, "I don't like the look of this. We're going to need a biopsy." He pressed the scanner against the suspect area for a few more long seconds, set the wand back on the sounder, and offered again, "I just don't like the looks of this. Try to be prepared for bad news." Then he added with faint optimism, "Of course, 9 times out of 10 the biopsies are negative, so let's hope for the best."

Alexandria, who is Caucasian, turned whiter than the pallid bust of Pallas. Me, I'm Latino, but I'm pretty sure I paled up myself. This was not the news we wanted to hear.

Biopsy day. I was there, of course, but had to leave for the waiting room as soon as I saw the needle sink into her bare and beautiful right breast. Let's face it. Alex is tougher than I will ever be, often strong-willed to the point of annoyance. She's been through a lot, including a sex-change surgery that would have killed a man. I wasn't there for that procedure, though I read a book called *Journal of a Sex Change* to try to understand what was involved.

I accept that such treatment is needed though I don't really understand the why. For example, Alex never says that she "became a woman" after surgery. She insists she was born a woman but needed help with the female part. From what I know of her, and I know a lot, Alex is a deep-girl fem despite her toughness. She's petite, looks naturally beautiful to everyone, and I never suspected she was trans when I first met her. In fact, I thought she was joking when she spilled the beans on our second date, but then she showed me her original birth certificate and high school graduation photo. It was Alex, all right, yet at the same time, it was not.

After I quit stuttering I croaked, "Why haven't you changed that birth certificate, Alexandria?"

She replied, "Cause I was born in Tennessee."

Apparently, that was explanation enough. I later checked and found that Tennessee had passed a special law specifically prohibiting transsexual individuals from changing their birth certificates. A couple of weeks later, when I decided that Alexandria was one hundred percent Alexandria and that her sex change didn't make one iota of difference to me, I wanted to sue Tennessee in federal court to get her birth record amended as it is routinely done in the majority of other states, but Alex put her foot down. "Tennessee bureaucrats," she said flatly, "are irrelevant in the scheme of my life, and I will not debate my femininity in *their* courts." Six months later, I asked her to marry me.

Anyway, she had her biopsy and came to get me in the hospital waiting room. She bragged, "I was positioned so that I could see the whole procedure on the video screen," she said. "It's amazing to watch a needle pass into flesh and poke around." She raised her left eyebrow and added in an excellent Spock imitation, "Interesting."

Told you she was tough. At her description, I again almost fainted.

The hospital called Alex four days later. The representative asked her, "Do you want the biopsy results by phone, now, or would you and your husband prefer to come to the office?"

"No need to wait," she said. "Shoot."

They did. Alex had "infiltrating lobular carcinoma." Breast cancer.

She immediately called me, reported the news, and then let go with sobs over the phone. It's rare that she cries, so I canceled my afternoon appointments (one drunk-driving case and another for juvenile shoplifting) and went home. I held Alex late into the night.

An MRI would be required to assess the tumor grade and size so that doctors could recommend treatments. At minimum, a lumpectomy would be needed. Alexandria refused to consider anything beyond that, and I knew that the situation was bad. Alexandria's breasts were part of her identity. This is true for most women, of course, but exceptionally true for Alex. She was fortunate that hormone therapy had resulted in a curvy B+ cup size, and she had never needed or wanted implants. Alex was proud that she grew breasts herself, and my wife would have a devil of a time allowing a surgeon to cut into that part of her body, which had nothing to do with physical pain. After all, few surgeries are as excruciating as constructing a vagina from a penis. But for Alex, a mastectomy or lumpectomy would offer layers of psychological discomfort—somehow peeling away her femininity.

Another big issue. Doctors told Alexandria to stop taking estrogen immediately. Her cancer was an estrogen receptor, which is generally a good sign as far as treatability, and they wanted to cut off the disease's stimulus. Then the oncologist added one more thing: "I'm also prescribing Arimidex, an estrogen blocker."

At that, my wife bolted. "No!" she said. Not a small "no," but an in-your-face go-to-hell "No." She added, "Estrogen is the elixir of life. For me, it *is* life. I will *never* take your blocker poison."

Neither I nor the doctors could persuade her otherwise.

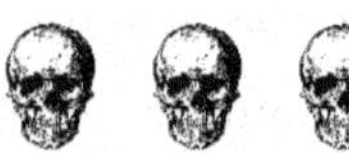

A week later we met with the cancer-wing surgeon to discuss recommended treatment. The doctor said, "The MRI shows a second, smaller tumor below the first, and both have irregular borders with small tendrils reaching into the breast tissue. But the good news is there's *no evidence* of cancer in the left breast or that it has spread beyond the tumor site."

Alexandria had started to cry silently. I doubt she was even aware of it. I didn't even know until I saw the doctor hand her a tissue.

The doctor continued, "We'll check the lymph nodes

when we excise the tumor, but this is a highly treatable cancer. It was caught early. It is localized. Your prognosis is excellent."

Alex did not respond immediately but finally asked the fatal questions. "What about the surgery. How much?"

The doctor answered, "Oh, don't worry about that. Your insurance will cover the costs."

"No," said my wife, "How much surgery?"

The surgeon, a compassionate woman who had dealt with this issue many times, said, "Because of the double-tumor configuration and the irregular borders, everyone agrees you should have a right-side mastectomy."

"Why can't you do a small lumpectomy?" asked Alex.

"Believe me," said the doctor, "if I tried to do a lumpectomy, it would look worse than a mastectomy with breast reconstruction. And don't worry," she added. "We can do the reconstruction while you're still under the general anesthesia."

Alexandria shook her head, and I interjected before anyone else could speak again. "We'd like a second opinion because my wife is reluctant to have a mastectomy." Alex and I had looked at photos of breast reconstruction three nights before; she was disappointed in the apparent cosmetic results, but also told me, "Even if they looked normal, I would never sacrifice my real body for an unfeeling surgical lump."

"I understand your reluctance," said the doctor to both of us, "and I suspected as much when Alex refused the estrogen blocker. Out of concern for Alex, I checked with two other board-certified practitioners. They arrived at the same conclusion. Mastectomy is the prescribed treatment."

The doctor paused and then added with compassionate professionalism, "Breast cancer is rare in trans women, though when it happens, psychological barriers to treatment, especially mastectomies, seem more intense. But please, Alexandria, we are working to save your life. You're a young, intelligent woman. Cancer can kill you. Allow us to kill it, instead."

"No," she said with an alarming certainty.

"Thank you, doctor," I interjected. "Alex will need time to think about this. It's a lot to take in all at once."

"I understand," she said, "and, of course, I must respect your decision. But keep in mind that the cancer is growing and will not stop unless we stop it. We should act as soon as possible to enhance survivability."

"I am *acting*," said Alexandria, standing to leave. "I am acting to save my soul." For Alex, having genital surgery and not having a mastectomy served the same purpose.

When we got home from the surgeon's office, Alexandria immediately called the hospital's cancer-unit coordinator and put their conversation on speaker so I could hear. "Hi, Janet, this is Alexandria Cerrillo," she said. "I've evaluated all of the information from the oncologist and surgeon, et al. You may inform everyone that there will be no mastectomy on this body. There will be no estrogen blockers. If they can figure out a treatment plan that doesn't involve that kind of mutilation, I'll listen and reconsider. Otherwise, I'll ask for pain meds when I need them—and I assume I will need them down the road—but this girl will not sacrifice her femaleness."

Janet didn't sound surprised or even particularly alarmed, and I supposed she often heard initial protests from cancer patients. I mean, what woman would *want* a mastectomy?

"Mrs. Cerrillo," said Janet with a gentle deference, "I know how you feel. Two years ago, I was faced with a similar diagnosis, except that my cancer was stage three in both breasts. After two days of prize-winning self-pity, along with a continuous flood of tears that made my eyes sting, I authorized removal of my breasts and three months of chemo. The reconstruction wasn't perfect, but I chose to live, and I'm hoping you will, too. You just talked with the doctor. Give yourself a few days to grieve. All of us here want you to live a long life."

Alexandria did not raise her voice. "I am not you. I suffered for several lifetimes during my childhood—just as you would have if your parents had tried to make a man out of you. And I know many things about doctors, too. One lovable family physician told me to 'do the world a favor and commit suicide' when I first came out as trans. You're *almost* asking me to do the same thing. That aside, I believe your doctors are caring and sincere. But they don't know what being a *visible* woman means to someone like me, someone so badly deformed at birth that people thought she was a boy. Well, Janet, I corrected that impression. Don't expect me to un-correct it."

"Alexandria, please, you're right that I don't fully understand your feelings, but I do know that the price I paid to live was worth every cut and stitch, every vomiting marathon after chemo, every burn from the radiation gun. It's incredibly important to be alive, and I'm sure you'll feel much the same way down the road. And by the way, if any doctor had ever told a patient to kill herself in my presence, that doctor would immediately find my foot in his crotch."

Alex smiled for the first time that day. "Thanks, Janet. I believe you, and I love you for what you've shared about yourself. But it won't affect my decision."

I quite suddenly felt irrelevant in this discussion.

"Listen, hon," continued Janet, "I'm going to call you after you've had time to let everything sink in; and beware of the internet information because a lot of it is just plain bad. But it's wrong to sacrifice your life because of some socially constructed notion of what a woman ought to be. This disease will kill you. Let us help!"

Alexandria lost her short-lived smile. "You're sweet, Janet, and I can't speak for anyone else who might refuse this surgery, but there are things worse than death. That's why transsexuals undergo the physical and social tortures of sex reassignment."

Janet, who initially struck me almost as tough as Alex, began to choke with emotion. Now, the roles reversed, and my wife tried to comfort the treatment coordinator.

"I'm sorry, Janet," said Alex. "Life has made me a little too blunt at times. Please do call me in a couple days. Maybe I'll have changed my mind."

It doesn't happen often, but I can always tell when Mrs. Alexandria Cerrillo is lying.

It was a week later that I walked into the bedroom to find my wife crying into her pillow. I had never seen this kind of demonstrative sorrow in all the time I had known Alex; in fact, I would have sooner expected to find a Navy SEAL bawling because the water's too cold as to find my wife crying alone in the bedroom.

I quietly approached and sat on the bed to comfort her.

She looked up and said, "Oh, honey, I don't want to die!"

"You're not going to," I replied, stroking her hair. "Cancer treatments are better than ever, and your prognosis is excellent. We're going to have a long, long life together."

"That's what I thought when I married you. And I was so happy. I mean, because I'm trans, I never expected to find a husband. Most men treated me like garbage once I told them. But then you came along...and even after you knew...you asked to marry me."

"And I got lucky that you said yes." This sent her into cat wails again, and she re-buried her face into the pillow. "I'm still lucky," I said.

Finally, when she stopped crying long enough to lift her head and take a clean breath, she added, "But you don't understand—you're too innocent, too loving. There are very few MTFs that have solid marriages. Social pressures are against us. Sometimes families even break up an otherwise happy union when they find out the wife is trans. Against the odds, I not only found a wonderful and loving husband, but found *you*, a man who could have picked from among the most beautiful natural females, a normal woman who could have given you children, who...."

I stopped stroking her hair and snapped, "Stop it!" I shouted. "I have never felt like slapping you until this moment. You are my wife. I love you. So knock off this *normal woman* crap. You're way above normal—smart, stable, ambitious, and beautiful. I meant it when I said I got lucky. How could you doubt me!?"

She flopped face down into the pillow. Her shoulders heaved. For the first time since her diagnosis, it occurred to me that she might actually refuse treatment. Down deep, I assumed that Alexandria would choose life against a mastectomy. My own eyes began to water. I realized I could lose her forever.

Then, within another minute, Alex turned off the tears, sat up in bed, and wiped her face with a tissue. "Well," she said, "I suppose I should be grateful for the time we've had—and the time we should have over the next year or two."

"Let's try for the next five decades," I suggested, now desperate.

"Seems unlikely unless the cancer cures itself," she said with a familiar resolve. "I won't let them mutilate my body."

Then Alex walked into the master bathroom, closed the door, and emerged five minutes later with clear eyes and light evening makeup.

"Where shall we go for dinner?" she asked.

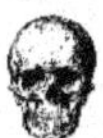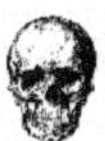

Over the next three weeks, I pleaded with Alex to change her mind and undergo the recommended treatments. She would not waver. "No" meant "no."

Janet also tried to persuade her.

"Look," responded Alex into the speaker phone, "if you can come up with a sure-fire treatment that allows me to keep my breast, I might consider it."

Janet did not pull her punches. "Nothing is sure-fire when it comes to cancer, but with a mastectomy and chemo, your chances are excellent. Ninety-four percent of patients with your disease are cancer free 10 years after treatment. Those are damned good odds. And life is more important than a few leftover scars and tissue numbness."

Alex replied, "I know you mean well, Janet, but until age 22, I tried to live with a deformed body. It didn't work. I won't ever try again."

Janet replied, "Many women have mastectomies. Some have hysterectomies at the same time, and they are still women afterwards. They know it, too."

"Sure," said Alex. "They knew it when they were two

years old or ten or twenty, but I am different. And I will not allow one ounce of my hard-earned womanhood to be stolen from me. Natural-born females can absorb that kind of loss. I can't."

Janet gave up for the moment. "Mr. Cerrillo," she said to me over the speaker. "Keep talking to this girl. Maybe you can help her to see reason, and I don't want her to make a deadly mistake. Once cancer metastasizes, it's difficult to recall. Talk to her!"

"I'll do my best," I said. And I did for many months.

I take red carnations to Alex's gravesite every Saturday. She loved flowers, especially carnations, and it does me good to visit the cemetery and talk with my wife.

I had the gravestone carved to meet Alex's specific request, which she assured me contained not a hint of humor. I suppose not, but I don't really like it, and I've seen people chuckle when they walk past her resting place:

Here Lies Alexandria Cerrillo
A Cancer-Killed Woman
Who Died with Her Boobs On

I have never known a love as warm and deep as I had with Alexandria. Unfortunately, there was one thing she loved more than me or carnations or even life itself. She loved being a woman. That's what killed her.

In the end, I realize that I can't really fault her choice, though I miss her terribly, because I loved *her* exactly as she was. So I try to accept her overwhelming femininity as an integral part of the emotional package that bound us together. Expecting her to be less of a woman in spirit would be like expecting her to be less Alexandria in existence. And even with the pain medications that helped her bear the last excruciating months of her illness, she never questioned the suffering. She would just take another pill and say, "There are worse things. Much worse."

I believe I suffered more than she did the final weeks but never told her. Could I scold her for loving what she had worked so hard to become? Still, a part of me wonders whether it was the love of being a woman or the hatred of being perceived as a man that destroyed her. Doesn't really matter at this point. One or the other killed her, and almost killed me, too. Alexandria Cerrillo was the most serious woman I have ever known

Before leaving the cemetery this Saturday, I carefully arranged the carnations in front of her headstone, turned slowly, and walked toward my car. Monday morning at 9:00 a.m., I would be in Superior Court, fighting the petition of Alexandria's father to exhume her body and rebury it under her male birth name—Alexander Stephens. I promised my wife that this would never, never happen—and it won't. For I am a most serious husband.

broken poem

by Ayodele Nzinga

this poem
is broken
like bread
for people
starving
4 mental groceries
broken
like paradigms
&
prom queens
once dimes now
sub past primes
broken
like banks
homes
& the backs of the poor
broken like
former heroes
broken like

law
& concepts of justice
just us
singing softly
talking about rights
under broken street lights
this poem is
broken
like lovers promises
& the spirit of captured
warriors
carved and eaten by
assimilation
broken
like capitalism in America
communism in Russia
like systems that have
rusted
turning savage
eating the old
breaking the young
like bread crumbs
broken to find the way home
broken
like dreams of the oppressed
pressed into projects
asylums without asylum
no Ellis island
incarcerated at a furious pace

Denial Kills

broken
like shoe laces
on boots that can't be
pulled up
no feet to stand on
broken
like this
poem
is broken
like yokes
&
camels backs
the hearts of faithful women
& wild horses
like cane
on backs
like skin
worn too thin
like cycles
& womb water break
giving birth to
wholeness
this poem is
broken
like horizons
& new sun
broken like
glass ceilings
crashing
onto crystal stairs

broken like
necks
& covenants
the wings of doves
shot guns
religious fast
the english of immigrants
& rappers grammar
broken like
the will of the weak
broken
like morning on
a new day
borders
boundaries
& margins
broken
wide open
like
a meadow
run here with
razors
cutting breaking
smashing cussing
building broken
things to break
broke things
this poem is
broken

The Original Confession Shop and Café

by T. J. Berg

Anna clutched her ten euros, staring at the door, wondering what she might confess. Above her, the sign glared in red on a black background. The red-light district had many such shops, but the reviews on this one, which declared itself *The* Original Confession Shop and Café, rated it as the best--at least in Anna's price range. Whether it was really the original or not, she couldn't say. Hyperbole wasn't much affected by the limiters. Outright lying, yes. Some creative exaggeration, no.

She studied her ten. Something to do with that? An adventure maybe, thieving and daring-do. Or even just something simple and really mean, like snagging it out of one her dorm-mates' wallets. Or her mother's purse. Wouldn't that be a terrible thing to confess? Stealing from your own mother. What would she think? What would her mother have done to her? Thrown her out? (Would the limiters allow that?) Ten euro was groceries for several days. Her mother worked hard for that money (she would say). Would the confession include consequences? Anger and shouting, some wonderfully emotional display?

For ten euro, Anna hoped so. It was supposed to buy a "full package."

A man brushed by her and entered the shop. A blast of warm air spilled across her face, bringing the scents of coffee and sweat. Was that what she expected sin to smell like? Anna caught the door as it swung in then crossed the threshold. The translucent curtains thinned the already meager winter light so it hardly competed with the lamps, muted beneath their red and gold shades. Most of the customers had come alone, though a couple occupied a comfortable couch beneath a picture-- carefully edited with sweeps of painted cloth--of a group of frolicking nudes.

Her cousin Nana told her that when the limiters first came to the EU from the US twenty years ago, they promised they would only be used to curb violent crime. But the growing Nationalist elements pushed and pushed, using fears of terrorism by people outside the EU to keep unlimited visitors out, and later to limit more and more activities to keep everyone in line with "EU values" because so many "foreigners" had already established themselves. Anna asked her cousin what EU values were, but Nana only shrugged. "Whatever the government decides they are," she said. Then she had flipped open her art history book and waved an eloquent hand over the photos. Nudity and violence mingled on the pages. It wasn't technically limited to look at, but it generated discomfort. Her throat tightened. It was as if she'd been offered a plate of raw chicken to dine on, pinkish fluids pooling on the plate. Stomach clenched, she had closed the book. Nana laughed, but sweat dampened her hairline.

The Confession Shops were barely legal, even in Amsterdam. Anna was glad she was getting a chance to experience one before they were shut down, as her cousin often said they would be, eventually. Her mother said so too, tight-lipped and disapproving. "People want to do crimes," she would say. "And they can't." She would scratch her cheek with one nervous finger, as she always did whenever she was provoked to talk about the limiters.

Nana was involved in a lot of politics. Her mom didn't approve of Nana either, and didn't like them meeting, but now that Anna was at university, there wasn't much her mother could do about it. Limits involving parental obedience were complicated, but they ended at eighteen.

"Were you looking for a table?" A young man approached, neatly dressed, lip fringed with a brown mustache. It made her think: *Fragile.* As if a sparrow alighted there, trembling for purchase on the narrow rim of his lip.

He wore a name tag that said, "Lucas."

Anna tried to hide her sudden panic. Was she really going to do this? Why hadn't she planned in advance? Now she was just stuck, trembling and sweating and probably smelling. "First time?" Lucas asked. He gestured toward a table in the corner. "Just sit and enjoy some coffee. Call up the menu at the table. You can use the interface there to choose a confession, or we can chat and come up with something together. All right?"

He guided Anna to a table. Its glossy surface came to life with a tap of his finger. She sunk into thick cushions as the menu, gold and red on a black background, faded through options. Shoplifting was one of the first. Her mother told her once that she'd thought about stealing, but hadn't needed a limiter to know it was bad. "I wonder that your generation will understand that good and evil are a choice. Never have that decision to make. Just to have it made for you." She'd followed that with a barely audible mutter, but Anna heard it all the same. "It's no wonder you're so pathetic." Would she think she was pathetic now? Sitting here, at the Confession Shop? Gazing at all the illicit crimes the limiters prevented, drinking in the possibilities? Had her mother ever stepped out of her limited little life and considered confessing a crime?

The young man returned with a pot of coffee, the gleaming silver arch of its spout reflecting a line of red light. It sat on a clear tray with a porcelain tea cup, the aging pattern of pink roses as faded as dusk.

He poured her a cup, smiling. He looked about her age, and she liked his smile, even if his mustache was a bit silly. "So, did you want some help with your selection? You're welcome to do it in private of course, but it is a bit more exciting when someone else is along for the ride."

"Have you?" Anna asked, staring into the blackness of the coffee.

His smile twisted slightly. "Oh the things I could confess," he said. His voice held a slight tease.

The menu started with little things, thievery, vandalism. Then more violent things, fights and brawls and protests, larger acts of destruction. You could smash a car window, grab the driver by the hair, tug them out onto the street, give them a kick in the gut, then steal their car. You could joyride, break speed limits, crash the car--into an embankment or another car or even, she saw, through a shop window. People would be hurt. She tried to feel if that would give her a thrill, to confess such an act, but no, hurting a bunch of strangers, hurting even one stranger, offered no temptation.

Lucas, she thought, looked relieved. Some tightness in his hand and voice dropped away when she'd said, "No, nothing like that."

You could destroy parking meters, peek in bathroom stalls, light a firework inside a courthouse.

"Where do they come up with these?" she asked.

"There's writers. And people often make custom modules and volunteer to leave them as a shared experience." He paused. "But we make each unique, to the individual. They're never exactly the same."

"So, people actually did these things though, once."

"Some of them. I guess we're a lot safer now, huh?" His voice sounded sincere, but his mouth quirked into the kind of sarcastic smile that Nana often displayed.

"You can mouth off to the police? Or evade curfew? Rob a bank ..." None of it sounded like what she wanted though.

Before her dad disappeared, when she'd overheard him telling her mom that his limiter was malfunctioning, she remembered him saying, "I know I can do anything now. But why would I? What would Anna think if her dad went off and committed some crime?"

Her parents had been in the kitchen, Anna standing just outside, hesitating at first because the kitchen stank of boiled eggs, then because she'd wanted to hear more. Her mother muttered, "But you want to, don't you?" Anna hadn't heard her dad's reply. When she'd come into the kitchen finally, her mother stood on the far side from her dad, hand clenched tight around the handle of a small pot.

It was a few days later that her dad hadn't come home from work. Her mom had told her, arms stiff at her sides as she stared into the dishwater, "He's gone to the hospital." Then she'd scratched at her cheek until it bloomed red. Her hand stilled on the red cheek like a memory.

And weeks later, when he still hadn't returned: "He's abandoned us. Forget about him."

Her mom couldn't lie, right? The limiters prevented outright lies. But stretched truth? Could "abandon" have bent itself around the limiters?

"So," Lucas said. "Are you feeling like an act of rebellion? I'm not getting violent crime off you. There's a lot of adventurous crimes. Cat burglary--that was a thing once. People creeping around buildings, up walls and in windows and stuff, to steal things." He topped up her coffee from the pot. She hadn't realized she'd even drunk some. "There's sex things," he said. "The illicit kind. You can sell yourself even. That's what the red-light district used to be. And we allow rape here. Not all the shops do."

She shook her head. Why would she rape someone or sell herself? It wasn't as if any of it would really happen but she'd *think* it happened. Why would she want to remember doing something like that? "Do a lot of people ask to rape someone?" she asked.

Lucas put a finger to his lips. "We aren't allowed to discuss it."

"People are messed up." Then, with a rush, all the most horrific things that people used to do splashed through her brain like a waterfall--rape, child rape, hitting children, hitting wives, blowing up buildings, killing each other. You could do all that here. But no one was hurt. As if he could see that flood of thoughts drowning her, Lucas put his hands across the table, tapping the menu to let it fade.

"Most of what people ask for is small," he said. "And a lot of violent things, it's true. But there's a lot of little things--graffiti and telling off teachers or parents or police, protesting. Do you know, I scrawled *Limiters Suck* on the wall of the police station." He laughed. "In retrospect, I bet they agree. Kind of put them out of a job. There's hardly even any terrorism anymore."

"Well, they did help my neighbor get her car out of a

ditch."

They laughed together now.

"Sometimes though," he said, "it's the little forbidden things that are the most satisfying. And there's no getting rid of the memory. For people that choose a horrible crime to confess, that's never going away."

Small rebellions. Graffiti. Protest. Egging the Office of Limitation. Throwing a shoe at a politician. Anna realized something. It was something she thought even Nana, with all her history books and politics, hadn't realized. "They're never going to make this illegal, are they?" Anna said. "They'll keep acting like they will, but they need this. It keeps us--quiet. So we can all confess to our little rebellions."

Lucas raised his palms in the air, swept the menu clean from the table. "Do you want to go?" he asked. "Save your money?"

"No," she said. Then, voice low, "I want to kill my mother."

He swept a forefinger across the table, tapped a few places. "I'm required to inform you of the risks of cognitive dissonance in the case of murder of a person you know and may encounter again." His face had become professional. No more playfulness. "If you'll present your wrist, I can upload our recommendations for necessary adjustment strategies."

"I never want to see her again anyway," Anna muttered as they connected wrists, set permissions, and shared files.

Lucas swept and tapped the table until a menu appeared with an array of weapons. "You can choose your weapon, location, style, struggle level of victim." His voice had become distinctly cold, though she could tell he was trying to hide his disapproval beneath his professional polish. "There's a database of historical murders that you can choose from, if you prefer."

Anna slid her coffee cup clear to the edge of the table, though it wasn't truly in the way of any of the menu options. Her fingers hovered over knives and guns, swords and poisons, ropes thick and thin, each with drop down menus for further options. She could squish her with a car or electrocute her in the bathtub with a toaster. There was a sliding bar that allowed you to choose the amount of blood, the length of time it takes to die, the suffering level. One menu read "Torture Options." She let her finger hang there while Lucas attempted not to fidget. She sat back. She closed her eyes and pictured her mom's cheek, bright red from a slap.

"What about custom modules? I don't see what I want on here."

"I can help you generate a custom confession." His hands grasped one another, let go. He swiped the table clear again. "So, how would you like to murder your mother then?" he asked.

Anna's lips pressed against her teeth. "Can she be told?" she asked, wavering a moment.

Lucas's chin tipped down then up, stiff like his head was on a lever. "As per your psychological protection agreement, the victim can be notified."

"And she'll--she'll know how I did it?"

"If you want to release that information."

Yes, she thought. *Yes.* "Then I'd like to turn her into the authorities for subversion of her limiter."

Why the River?

by Zach Murphy

Shannon sat in her tattered recliner chair
Scowling, cheesy infomercials on her television.
Four years since the Mississippi River took her son.
Gus was a freshman and victim of the toxicity
Still desperate to fit in.

Shannon's fight for justice fell into the cracks of despair until her cries went completely unheard. She cursed the university for its disgusting negligence and its audacity to ask people for money. And she cursed the river for carrying on as if nothing had happened.

2:00 AM, Shannon took her pickup truck
Her passengers black paint, a dirt-covered brick, and ladder.
The paint, the ladder and the brick from the back.

She ran toward the house and hoisted the ladder against the front of the balcony. She took the paint and drenched the Kappa Sigma symbol in black. Then she wrote *"Leave before it's too late. I'm gonna haunt you until your world knows no happiness"* and tossed it into the office window. The glass shattered like Shannon's life when she first heard the news about her son, and she sped off with an ear-piercing screech.

Picking a shard of glass out of her boot,
Parked under a shadow
Across the road toward the river's edge.
Streetlights flickered with secrets to tell.
Was he alone when he wandered off.
Toward the river - did he even decide at all?
Just slipping and stumbling into the river,
His pain soaked to oblivion..

Shannon looked out at the river. The moon reflected upon its rolling ripples. She tossed the paint bucket into the water, certainly with no remorse for what she'd just done. She closed her eyes as the early morning breeze whipped around and the cold water splashed onto her weathered face, for the first time a tiny sliver of her soul felt alive.

The Judgment of Josephine K

by Joanna Michal Hoyt

Someone must have made a mistake in processing Josephine K's documents. Surely her security clearance and her bank balance should have been more than sufficient to ensure her a sleeper car of her own, but here she was in a cramped seat against an uncovered window.

Such a strange, narrow train—only one seat between aisle and window on each side. She didn't care for window seats. As the golden wall drew nearer and the press of people outside the train blocked most of the light, she wished she could stop them looking at her like that. At least the glass seemed soundproof, blocking out whatever they were saying.

Was it her fault they didn't have tickets even for this economy train (for such it must have been)? Was it her responsibility to take care of the babies they'd popped out and now insisted on waving at her? One of the children held up to her window was unmistakably dead. Shameless, to exhibit him — it — like that. And yet they looked at her as if they expected her to do something.

People had looked at her that way before, when... She wasn't going to think about that. This train was taking her away from all the worry and negativity.

The people outside the train were running at her. No, running parallel to the train, looking back over their shoulders. What was coming behind them? She didn't want to know. She didn't look back. The view ahead was not altogether reassuring. A woman staggered, swayed, checked just short of the rail line, holding up another child.

She wasn't showing this one to Josephine. She thrust it up past the window. For a moment her torso blocked Josephine's view. When the woman's feet hit the ground again her arms were empty. Then she gathered herself for a flying leap...

And fell, twisting at a terribly wrong angle. Behind her someone else fell. People shoved. People appeared to be screaming. At first there was no sound. Then Josephine heard an ugly strangled cry—through the glass? No, she'd made it herself. She shut her mouth, looked around at her fellow passengers. The thin man with the facial tic who sat opposite her looked away from her just as she looked at him. The beautiful overdressed woman behind him kept staring at her.

The conductor hurried down the aisle. "Nothing to worry about," he said in a rapid automatic voice. "Best to keep your eyes to the aisle as your boarding documents made clear the glass is bulletproof as well as soundproof you are perfectly safe in here."

"She put a child on top of the train," Josephine K said, to cover for the fact that she was quite unable to recall having received any boarding documents. "They're trying to smuggle people into our destination."

"Can't have that," the man with the tic said, nodding—nodding, Josephine thought, a little too rapidly.

"Poor things, it's a shame," the glamorous woman said vaguely, turning her attention to the contents of her purse. Josephine watched that search from the tail of her eye, thinking that if she could see the other woman's boarding documents it might help her to remember her own. But the woman, after pawing through the purse several times, merely extracted a mirror and a comb. Josephine's fossicking in her own carry-on bag failed to turn up any documents. It wasn't only for camouflage that she extracted a roll of antacids from the bag and ate two.

"Not to worry," the conductor gabbled. "The Pearl Gates were designed specifically to accommodate this railway service with all possible security precautions there is no more than an inch of vertical clearance still best to keep your eyes to the aisle as we enter estimated arrival in less than five minutes."

For an ugly moment Josephine thought of the infant and the one-inch vertical clearance. Then she occupied herself, more sensibly if not more comfortably, with the question of boarding documents. She glanced again at her fellow passengers. The woman applied makeup with an unsteady hand. The man patted his pockets, his eyes darting. He didn't pull anything out. The man in the seat ahead of him bent down, feeling under his seat, and sat back up empty-handed after making quite a business of tying his shoe.

The train stopped when the glitter of the wall ahead filled half the sky. The public announcement system wheezed to life; it was unintelligible as most of its kind, but Josephine was almost sure she heard "security check" and "passengers will present..."

Josephine was in the second row from the front of her train-car. The tall blonde woman in the seat ahead said, in a high inconsequential voice, "Such a silly thing, but my boarding documents, I seem to have... well, not to have..."

The conductor's voice was toneless as ever. "Not to worry ma'am about a little thing like that. No need to inconvenience yourself. Just give the passphrase."

Once again the ticcy man looked away from Josephine just as she looked at him.

"I belong in here," the blonde woman said slowly. "They belong out there."

"Excellent ma'am all in order now sir..."

The man ahead of the ticcy man repeated the phrase in quick irritable tones. Then added, as though in spite of himself, "But if an impostor... if one of them got on here, couldn't they say the same thing?"

"Oh no no sir certainly not in the right way," the

conductor said

Josephine turned her head away in case she looked nervous. She saw a skinny child in travel-stained clothing leap past her window, catch hold of something above, and swing up and out of sight. One of the child's worn sandals fell past the window, leaving her briefly glimpsed foot bare, blistered and bloody.

"No," Josephine said, thinking of the clearance. Couldn't they see...?

"No what?" the ticcy man demanded.

Josephine clasped her hands together to keep them from making any telling gestures. "No, of course an impostor could not speak with the requisite degree of self-possession," she said austerely. When the conductor turned toward her she managed to pronounce the pass-phrase in professional tones. It seemed to her that the conductor smiled unpleasantly; then she reflected that she'd never liked his smile from the beginning, which meant either that he had doubted her from the beginning or that the expression was habitual and had nothing to do with her. At last, he went on to the next row of seats.

Later—it felt like a long time later– the train began to move again. There was a flash of gold, a softer pearly gleam, a burst of harp music almost loud enough to drown out a far less pleasant sound, and they were inside.

"Ladies and gentlemen, be so good as to step this way," the conductor intoned, opening a door. Josephine rose, wincing a little as she unbent her knees. How long had the train ride gone on? It had felt like an eternity. It couldn't have been.

Whatever doubts the train had raised in Josephine's mind about her destination were dispelled by the landscape into which she disembarked. She was at one end of a colonnade floored with lustrous green grass short and uniform as carpet. The tall columns were white, with hints of gold in the intricate ornamentation of their capitals. Down the middle of the columned aisle ran a white marble pathway on which beautifully dressed people walked. Beyond the columns on either side were banquet tables spread with gold-edged white tablecloths and set with fine gold-edged white china and good silver. More well-dressed people sat at the tables. No one ate. No one hurried. No one shouted. She finally had what she had worked for all those years before...

Her mind squirmed violently as it approached the thought of what had led to her boarding the train.

"Is something wrong?' She thought from the questioner's tone that perhaps she had missed the question the first time around. She glanced nervously at the questioner, a nondescript man in a resplendent suit.

"Nothing wrong," she said. "Maybe I'm a little motion-sick from the journey."

"Ah, but no one is sick here," he said. "Surely you can't be ill now that you've come to your just reward." There was something disconcerting in his smile. His left hand flicked a discreet gesture. Motioning to her? Or to someone else? She glanced back over her shoulder, saw a uniformed guard looking expressionlessly past or through her.

She turned back to the man in the suit, tried to smile. "Of course," she said. "Nothing to worry about here, I suppose."

"Hardly anything," he answered. "The occasional impostor, perhaps, but the security services take care of them." His eyes flicked away from hers. "We are thankful for our blessings, of course," he said, "and we deserve them. We want for nothing."

Josephine looked away too, trying to find the source of the faint chiming and the brief glow which had accompanied his words. Looking back at him, she saw his eyebrows rise inquiringly.

"I... What was that sound, that light? It was lovely," she added hastily, not wanting to give him any further cause to think her a discontented impostor.

"That would be the Wall," he said, nodding. "It is beautiful, isn't it? Our faith keeps it great."

"So when you praise it, it grows?" He nodded. "And..." She bit the rest of the question off, seeing what she took for a warning in his eyes. She was about to seek a graceful way of exiting the conversation when another, harsher sound caught her attention. "What was that?" she asked again, in a different tone.

"What?" he asked.

"I... I heard something. From outside, I think."

"You will find it better," he said, "not to think of such things." His tone was cold. His left hand flicked again, and this time she was sure that he was looking over her shoulder at the guard.

"I'm sure I will," she said as warmly as she could. Did she sound fake? "It's only that I'm new here. I'll learn, of course."

"Of course," he said. "That's all we ask of new arrivals. That they come with proper documentation, and that they assimilate properly. After all, if you want to come here, why make this place more like whatever you chose to leave behind?"

"Best not to think of such things," Josephine said demurely. "Surely those of us who are fortunate enough to belong here could never wish to think of anything but the safety and the blessings we enjoy." She heard the soft chiming again and saw the light. Yes, she'd make her way very well in this place. She could use the skills she'd learned in all those years of...

She wasn't going to think about that.

The well-dressed man nodded and stepped aside. Josephine strolled past him, smiling, noting the assured smiles of her fellow fortunate ones before discreetly glancing back to make sure the guard was not following her.

He was following her. Josephine fumbled in her mind for the pass-phrase and the tone that would make it convincing.

"What did you say?' the guard demanded, running forward.

"I only said we were lucky...I mean, blessed..."

Josephine babbled. But the guard ran past her.

Josephine looked where he was looking. The guard had stopped in front of the ticcy man from the train, who shifted from foot to foot and looked quite dangerously frightened and ungrateful.

"I, I just said, there's plenty of room in here," he stammered.

"What else?"

"I just said we could have taken that kid in," he gasped, his face turning white as the Pearl Gate. "The kid off the train roof. Instead of letting him die like that. We would have had room. That was all I said."

"Was it, now," the guard said. "And what did these people say?"

The people around him all began to speak at once. Josephine couldn't sort out which words went with which faces. Perhaps that was because the words and faces didn't seem to match. The faces were frightened. The words were trying not to be.

"I said, everyone who belonged here got here..." "I said, it's the mother's fault, putting him up there; what did she think would happen, and why didn't she get a ticket?" "I said, I can't imagine what you're talking about."

That last sentence was pronounced with great firmness. At once the gushing voices said, "That's what I said too, what I said too, such nonsense, what was he talking about?" The frightened faces nodded. It seemed to Josephine that the faces were all turning pale, draining of color and somehow of feature as well, that they were all mannequin faces, white and smooth as pearl under their smooth golden hair, white and smooth around their blue glass eyes. What did she look like? She didn't want to know.

"You saw it!" The ticcy man's face had gone purple. His dark eyes flickered nervously across the faces around him. His mousy brown hair stuck out in tufts. His hands and his voice shook. "You saw! His mother lifted him up onto the train, trying to get him in! And you saw when we came through the Pearl Gate! The one-inch clearance—that was for real! You saw!" His frantic eyes swept over the crowd, settling on Josephine.

"Did you see something?" the guard asked. It seemed to Josephine that his eyes stuck on her as well. She didn't know what to say... she didn't want... she didn't dare...

"I see something." The woman who spoke was blonde and fair as the others had become, but her hair was rougher, and her face was sharply individual, too bony for beauty, screwed up with—fear? courage? "I see what's happening to you all. To us all. Don't you know where we are?"

"We came through the Pearl Gate," the bright people around her said, their voices thinning and sweetening into unison. "We're where we belong."

"Maybe we do belong here, God help us," the bony woman said. "Maybe we all deserve to be in Hell. But is there no way out?"

"Hell?" Josephine echoed hoarsely.

"All of us, scared witless!" The woman's voice grew lower, rougher, stronger. "All of us, turning our heads away from the windows, lying to get in, lying so we could get to a place where we'd have to keep lying until we forgot how to do anything else. And before... We wouldn't have done that on the train, would we, if we hadn't spent our lives doing it? We've damned ourselves. I'll say it, if nobody else will. We're damned."

Josephine glanced over her shoulder again. Surely there had been a cracking sound, a dimming of the light. Surely the great Wall was not quite so high as it had been.

The bony woman seemed to think so too. "Look at the wall!" she crowed. "We can take it down! We can get out!"

"You're getting out, lady," the guard said. "You and this clown." He gestured to the ticcy man. "Two one-way tickets to the Outer Darkness. Clear out, the rest of you."

The porcelain people glided away. They were perfectly in step, though some of their hands shook slightly in different rhythms. None of them touched.

Josephine stood, fixed and staring, as the guard laid a hand on the bony woman's right elbow, on the ticcy man's left elbow, and conducted them toward the wall. The woman strode half a pace ahead of him. The man dragged and stumbled, seemingly unable to break free.

The guard didn't take them to the gate, but to the wall. Josephine, dimly remembering something from the stories she hadn't wanted to hear in her life before the train journey, expected him to turn them around and summon a firing squad. That didn't happen. He thrust them forward into the wall itself.

For a moment two holes opened like eyes in that

blank expanse. The woman hurried, and the man fell, through.

A wind blew in through the holes. How had Josephine not noticed how unmoving, how stale the air was inside the wall? Another fragment of memory shoved its way into her mind. *The wind bloweth where it listeth.* Who had said that? This wind carried a smell that was hot and complicated and alive, and a strange mix of sounds. What was going on out there?

She took a step toward the holes, trying to see. Caught the guard's eye.

"Never you mind," he said. "They got what they were asking for." He held a hand out—courteously gesturing her back, she thought, not moving to grab her; but that could change in an instant. Behind him the holes in the wall had begun to film over. Faint shapes of light were superimposed between her and the dimness beyond.

They weren't reflections. Glancing over her shoulder, she saw the bright colonnade and the porcelain people gliding away. Glancing ahead again, she saw too-well-remembered figures looking at her as though they still expected something from her after what she'd done and what she hadn't done.

There was Marta who'd cleaned the office building where Josephine worked–she still didn't want to remember at what--who used to compare notes on bird sightings with her; Marta whom she'd last seen staring out of her computer screen, tight-lipped and curl-shouldered between uniformed agents. Lettie had sent a link to the news story, and to a petition, and to a fund drive for Marta's kids (the oldest was seventeen, and would be looking after her little brothers, since they'd all been born in the States and weren't being taken away...)

Josephine deleted the email. It had nothing to do with her. She hadn't asked ICE to look into Marta's background. She hadn't voted to have Marta deported, just the criminal aliens and the traffickers. And what if Marta was really a criminal? It wasn't Josephine's job to make such judgments, or her place to interfere with the people who had that job and were doing it.

When Lettie forwarded another furious email saying that Marta had been found back in Honduras with her throat slit, Josephine went out to the liquor store, came home and drank in front of the mirror, staring at herself so as not to see Marta; staring until she thought she saw her cousin Shelley staring back at her out of the glass, at which point she turned away and was violently ill.

Now, staring at the filmed-over holes, Josephine saw herself and Shelley. Eleven years old, dancing in the pasture under the full moon as Shelley sang wild lovely songs of her own invention. Twelve years old, Josephine staring worriedly as Shelley argued out loud with herself, not looking at her cousin, and then hung her head and cried. Fourteen years old, in the high school halls: Shelley arguing with herself again; Tricia looking at Shelley with obvious disgust and then looking questioningly at Josephine; Josephine, frantic, torn between fear for Shelley and fear of Tricia and her lot, realizing too late that the struggle probably showed on her face and made her look like Shelley, opting to perform an exaggerated version of Shelley's distracted look and Shelley's shuffle, freezing when Shelley turned to see what people were laughing at...

Josephine closed her eyes. She didn't want to see all the repeats of that day, or to see Shelley's accusing stare, Shelley's face going blank.

The notice of Shelley's death – overdose? suicide?— had arrived six years later, when Josephine, doing nicely in college, hadn't seen her trailer-trash cousin for four years.

She looked back at the wall. It could hardly be worse than the images playing behind her closed eyelids.

The face that looked back at her was her own: lonely, haunted. To get outside, to reach Marta and Shelley as she should have done long ago, she'd have to walk through that reflection, she'd have to remember everything she'd done, she'd have to live with it. That was too much to ask.

"Look away," the guard said. "You belong in here, don't you?"

"No." Josephine spoke with a vehemence that surprised her. She didn't know if she was saving or condemning herself. "No. I don't belong here. Nobody does. I'm leaving. I'm going back to them. There has to be some way to make this better."

She stepped forward, hardly noticing how the Wall dimmed and shrank as she passed into the Outer Darkness.

It wasn't completely dark. The stars clustered close and thick overhead, and somewhere ahead a bonfire glowed. There were voices all around her, weeping, singing, in a raw rich harmony. She stared around her, stumbled. Someone took her gently by the arm and led her deeper into the gathering of her broken people.

Checking Out

by Simon J. Plant

A clatter resounds through the room as Marsha draws back the blinds. Daylight floods the room like an unwelcome guest. She squints and turns to the bed. "We'd better get going," she says. "Don't want to be late."

Marsha waits, standing over him. There's no reply from Harold, buried like an ostrich beneath the sheets. Thin, she thinks. He's always been a weed of a man. She rolls her eyes and steps into the bathroom.

In the shower she scrubs impatiently, then dries herself and picks out a simple outfit. Jeans. Sneakers. Grey sweatshirt.

She shakes two Advil into her palm and swallows them dry as she comes back into the room and sets a few next to Harold's side of the bed. "Going down to get us some coffee. While I do that, why don't you get in the shower. We should aim to leave by nine."

On his bedside table is an empty wine glass, and another (lip-stick smeared) lingers on the desk by the window.

"Harold?" When he continues to ignore her, Marsha feels a pang of irritation. Inconsiderate lout, she thinks. Willful, stubborn man. Five years of marriage counseling and nothing's changed—

A knocking sound cracks the morning open like an egg. She shuffles to the door and inches it open.

"Yes?" Marsha squints out at the woman but does not remove the security chain.

"Housekeeping," says the maid, a large dispassionate woman, bored eyes. Judging me, Marsha thinks.

"No thank you," Marsha says, "we're checking out. Can you come back?"

The maid grips her cart wordlessly and wheels it toward the next room.

Nate emerges from the motel's buffet disappointed. Really, he shouldn't be surprised. The continental breakfasts here are never good. But work has him traveling between Berkeley and Chico on a regular basis, and *this* motel is most convenient for Lily.

As he heads across the parking lot, he passes a woman in jeans and a grey sweatshirt. She's wearing large sunglasses and carries herself like one experiencing a hangover. Is that her, Nate wonders, the woman from last night? "Morning," he mumbles as she passes him. She doesn't respond, maybe doesn't hear him. She walks robotically toward the buffet, lips pursed.

Nate returns to his room to find Lily sitting on the bed smoking a cigarette and watching cartoons on an outdated tv. He shuts the door and points to the sign on the back of it. "Can't smoke in here."

"My bad." She drops the cigarette into a glass of water then brushes a hand through her tangle of blonde hair. "If they charge you, let me know. I'll subtract it next time."

Lily's attractive for a working girl, Nate thinks. Prettier than you'd expect. He hands her a bagel.

"Saw that woman just now…" he says. Lily had been unzipping his fly with her teeth last night when the argument upstairs had begun to escalate: loud voices, obstreperous and full of spite. He'd done his best to block out the noise; Lily wasn't cheap.

"That bitter married couple?" Lily says incuriously. Her eyes don't stray from the tv. "What about her?"

Stefanie wheels her cart to room 230 but her mind lingers on the woman in 229. She looked awful when she'd answered the door just now. A wraith of a woman. A vampire peering out of a cave. Mouth stained with red wine—

Or blood, Stefanie thinks morbidly.

And who speaks to their husband like that anyway, Stephenie wonders, recalling the snide little backhanded comments the woman had been making to the man as they approached the front desk with their suitcases. Stephanie had been watering the plants in the lobby when the terse couple arrived, and nothing about them had read "happily married". Be careful what you say, love, Stephanie had thought last night, eyeing the other woman with a kind of shrewd pity through the fronds of a parlor palm, one day you might wake up alone.

"Housekeeping," Stephanie trills. There's no answer from 230, so she lets herself in. Then: "Ugh." Dirty sheets cover the floor and hang off the backs of chairs. Half-empty bottles and stale pizza crusts are scattered everywhere and the particles of crushed Cheetos have been smooshed into the carpet like moon dust. People are disgraceful.

She sticks earbuds in her ears and gets to work. It's a thankless job. Uninspiring. Pays next to nothing. But Stefanie never went to college – technically didn't graduate high school. Has to do *something* to keep her girl in school. It's her life's mission not to let Dana turn out like her: fat and broke and depressed. Or worse. Like those girls Stephanie sees round here, checking-in to rooms with clearly married men.

This place attracts all sorts, Stephanie thinks. Should've named it The Fuck-It Inn. Artie would've got a kick out of that one.

She maneuvers herself on sore knees across the floor, scrubbing 230's bathroom tiles until they gleam like fresh enamels. She never wanted this. Never saw herself working this hard for a pittance. Would have been content in her role as a homemaker until Dana went off to college. Alas, when Artie stopped coming home, the bills did not.

She hears something then, and stops. Removes the

buds from her ears and listens.

Faintly, the furious voice of a woman through the wall. The woman from 229? Got to be. Her words are muffled but audible:

"Get up now, dammit! You lazy sack. Swear to god Harold, if you don't get up and shower I'm leaving without you!"

Marsha continues to stare through the crack in the door, past the banister, to the parking lot one flight down. In a flash, a vision of last night's events:

Marsha and Harold wheeling suitcases across cement. A travel-weary couple, irritable and stone-faced, checking in at a shabby road-side motel to escape the coming storm.

"Don't understand why we couldn't park here," Marsha had said. "Plenty of spots. See?"

"We're spending enough on this trip," was Harold's snappish response. "I'm not paying for parking. Gas ain't cheap and it's a long way to Santa Rosa. Your sister better be grateful."

Your sister, Marsha thinks. Never Georgette. Never Georgie. Always *Your sister*. Like Georgette is something only Marsha has to deal with. Like the fact that they're married does not link Harold to Georgette in some way. Like Marsha's sister, Marsha's *family*, means nothing to him. Cheap, ignorant man.

She'd gripped her suitcase until her palms hurt,

ground her teeth as Harold left a security deposit at the front desk and they made their way upstairs. Only then could the argument *really* begin, after wine had been uncorked and their edgy tongues loosened.

Marsha's eyes linger on the banister, the morning sun glinting off it like a blade. Muttering, she retreats into the room and shuts the door. She swipes her sunglasses from the bench, room-key and wallet. "Get a move on, Harold," she says and removes the safety chain, opens the door, steps outside. "I won't keep my sister waiting."

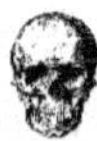

Nate reminds Lily what happened last night; the couple wheeling suitcases across the landing above, arguing; voices, muffled through the pop-corn ceiling, discernible even over the drumming rain.

"What's it concern you?" Lily says, then laughs. "You really shouldn't be giving advice to married couples." She tosses him his wedding band, which he's sure always to remove and leave on the bedside beforehand. He catches it and slides it on.

She checks the time. "Don't wanna rush you, but I got a DMV appointment."

As he counts the notes, Nate ponders the sounds he heard later, lying in bed with Lily breathing heavy beside him: embittered, piercing voices, the couple indefatigably hurling words at each other like kids hocking stones at passing trains. Never have me and Kendra argued like that, Nate thinks. Rarely in fact do Nate and Kendra argue at all. Kendra is a good christian woman and would not speak with such unhindered inhibitions. Though sometimes Nate wishes she would.

Marsha wants to dump both the steaming coffees on his head. She's been down to reception, got them both caffeine for the ride ahead, even considered buttering a slice of toast for the inconsiderate son of a fig. Now she's back and he hasn't even showered yet. Hasn't budged from his spot in bed.

The councillor often advises Marsha that patience is the tool to fix a broken marriage. Marsha thinks it's a crock. Marsha thinks what'd fix the marriage would be Harold pulling his finger out of his behind.

"Get up!" she says again. "Get up now, dammit! You lazy sack." She storms to the desk, dumps the coffees and begins snatching Harold's damp clothes from the floor. "Swear to god Harold, if you don't get up and shower I'm leaving without you!"

She pulls at the blanket. Then she shuts her eyes and screams.

"Six-hundred." Nate says, "Plus a little extra cos I was late."

"Thank you, Sir," Lily adopts a twee southern accent as she counts the cash, "pleasure doin' business with ya."

"Same time next week?"

"Sure." She pulls on a jacket and fluffs her hair.

Reapplies her makeup in the bathroom mirror. She kisses his cheek, steps over to the bed and gathers her belongings into a handbag. Then she turns back to him. "You wanna hold onto this until next time? It's easier to relax, you know, if you practice."

Nate blushes and looks down at his feet, refusing to look at the object in Lily's hand; far too real in the light of day. "No," he says. If Kendra found it, she'd have an aneurism.

"Okay," Lily says and flops it in her bag.

Nate feels a throb of excitement nonetheless. Then a jab of guilt. Kendra's not a bad wife, honestly. They have a beautiful life together; four lovely kids, big house, health insurance. Their sex life is decent, respectable, congenial. But sometimes a man's body needs... well, Nate decides not to analyze too closely what goes on in these rooms with Lily.

Besides, Kendra's sensibilities would take not to a topic so lurid as the stimulation of her husband's prostate. What Kendra doesn't know can't hurt her—

"They're at it again." Lily points at the popcorn ceiling. And now Nate hears it too; the woman upstairs is yelling like a banshee.

"*Get up now, dammit! You lazy sack...*"

Jeez, Nate thinks, whatever troubles Kendra and I have, at least we've never *spoken* to each other like that—

Then the woman begins to scream.

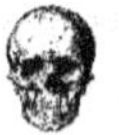  

Stephanie is still wearing the rubber gloves she dons

to scrub toilets when she bounds from 230 and onto the landing, heart pounding. That scream! she thinks. Bloodcurdling. Enough to wake the dead. Last time Stephanie heard a scream like that was two years ago when police called to inform her Artie wasn't coming home, and could she please pick a time convenient for her to identify the body. "Prepare yourself," the coroner had warned, "there's a lotta damage." His warning though did little to mitigate the horror when the sheet was pulled back to reveal a face flattened by an imploded windshield. Stephanie had realized the scream was coming from her own mouth only after her retreating back hit the cold wall behind her and she fell to the linoleum floor of the morgue. *Dana*, she'd thought, *how am I going to tell Dana?*

Stephanie stops now in the open doorway of 229, gloved hands gripping the doorjamb. The woman inside has stopped her screaming and has reverted to demanding her husband "—get the fig out of bed now or I'm divorcing you!"

"I knew right away," is what Stephanie will later tell police...

It all came back to Marsha in a flash.

Last night. She and Harold no longer speaking, the brave embers of their argument (any argument, really) only a light breeze from bursting to life like wildfire. Marsha guzzles her wine as Harold clicks aimlessly through channels on the tv. He's chewing loudly on a cheeseburger and she wants to hurl her glass at the wall. How many times has she mentioned the chewing? It turns me off, she had explained in many a past session. It's unattractive. It irritates me. Makes me want to kill you. The latter she had refrained from uttering in front of the councillor.

She mentions it now and he bristles visibly. He blurts a disgruntled defense to which Marsha responds with heated animosity. And just like that, they're off; dredging up old arguments like weary fishermen pulling garbage-filled nets from a polluted sea.

You always make a deal out of nothing.

You never listen to me.

You drink too much.

You have no ambition.

You're just like your mother.

You're pathetic.

You're morose.

And so on until Harold pushes to his feet and walks to the door. "Where are you going?" says Marsha.

"To get away from you."

Rain and wind smack Marsha's face as she follows him onto the landing. "That's the problem with you, Harold. You're a coward. Always have been."

"You know what, Marsha?" He turns back and throws up his hands. "I'm done."

Marsha blinks. "Done with what?"

"This!" A bolt of lightning ignites the sky behind him and in that moment she sees the resignation on his face, the defeat.

"You mean our *marriage?*"

"If you can call it that." He turns from her and plants his hands on the railing, oblivious to the rainwater soaking his clothes.

"Harold, you don't mean—"

"It's too hard." The fight has left him. He speaks rather with an earnestness that encroaches upon Marsha's nerves more so than his chewing or pigheadedness ever has. "It shouldn't *be* this hard."

No, Marsha thinks. You don't get away that easy. Whatever happened to *till death do us part*? "You can't bail when things get tough."

"Things haven't been good for a long time, Marsha. Can't you see this isn't working? We've done the counseling. But we just go round in circles. Don't you think it's time we hang it up? Maybe salvage what's left. Friendship..."

"Friendship?" Marsha barks an incredulous laugh. "We were never *friends*. That's not what marriage is. I don't even *like* you."

"Go our separate ways, then." He turns and walks toward the stairs.

"Where are you going?"

"To see if there's another room."

"Don't you dare walk away from me, Harold." Another flash of lightning injects into her a crazed strain of desperation, and she cries: "Don't leave me!" But Harold ignores her, maybe doesn't hear her over the storm. "I promised Georgette we'd be there, Harold!" Nothing. He keeps walking.

Her desperation petrifies into a cold fury.

Suddenly she's running for him, manic, reaching out clawed hands wanting to scratch and pull and rend at him, his stubborn face, his jowls, his scrawny shoulders, his spreading gut and unkempt, balding head; how many times did she suggest Rogaine? How many times did he deliberately ignore her?

Her hands meet his gangling form and she shoves him. He turns, skids on the slick landing, and his hip slams into the banister. His feet fly up and time stands still: Harold's body, for one fleeting moment, is tipped horizontally like a pencil balanced cleverly (precariously) upon the precipice of a finger. Then he's gone.

A cry as Harold falls. And then thunder swallows the world. But not loud enough for Marsha to miss the gunshot crack of Harold's head smacking the pavement below.

"Harold!"

Oh god, she thinks. No no no.

Feet beat upon the stairs and when she reaches the bottom she almost slips in a puddle of water. She rights herself, runs to where he landed – which ironically is a vacant spot between two cars demonstratively reserved for the handicapped.

He's unresponsive to her fretting hands. Blood mixes with the rainwater and rushes toward a drain.

"Harold!" she cries. "I didn't mean to—"

Thoughts crash through her mind and threaten to

freeze it like an overloaded server. You made me. You drove me to this. I love you. You wanted to leave me. You can't leave me. The councilor can fix us. We'll be okay. We'll talk about it at our next session and everything will be fine.

"Let's go to bed," she says, coming gingerly to her feet. "We'll talk in the morning..." She pretends she doesn't see the bits of shattered bone and gelatinous grey matter trying to wriggle free. Takes hold of his wrists instead. Despite a protest in her lower back, she drags him. Despite the tearing in her shoulder and another in her groin, she drags his slender body; easier considering her own is but a few pounds lighter. Her feet back carefully across the pavement, up the stairs, across the landing toward the door.

Inside 229, with Harold strewn limp on the bed, she applies the security chain and draws the blinds. Takes a spare towel from the bathroom and dresses Harold's head like a turban. "Wet out there," Marsha says, then laughs. "It's Georgie's Fortieth tomorrow. We can't show up looking like this. And you definitely can't go to bed in those clothes, Mister. You'll catch your *death*."

She begins peeling wet clothes from her body, then starts on his. "It's okay, Harold," she says as she props him up on a pillow beside her. "We don't have to talk about it. We'll talk tomorrow. Over coffee. Before check-out. When we're both sober and thinking clearly."

She pulls the blankets up, lays down beside him, and switches off the light.

Stefanie watches as the woman in 229 drags the naked man from the bed by one pale foot. Roughly the way a farmer might yank a bail of hay from a truck. She grunts and spits at the man, cursing him even as his body thuds uselessly upon the floor.

A chill seizes Stefanie's spine at the sight of the blood. The husband's side of the bed is *painted*. A great streak smeared like a hyphen down the sheet to the foot of the bed where the man is now crumpled, chin to chest, eyes half-lidded and sightless. A great open mess is the top of his balding head.

The woman stands over him, demanding he get up, get dressed, get in the car *now*. "I don't give a fig if you don't like Georgette, Harold. She's my sister and we're going!"

You Were Not Mine!

by Huda Tariq

Hey, do you know I waited for you, my days and nights
were betrayed
But you never came and it all delayed
Hey, do you know I was screaming your name
But you never came and I am the one to blame
Hey, do you know I want you with all the parts at my
zone
But you never came and it seems all gone
Hey, do you know I have saved you deep down in my
memories
But you never came and I am all okay it's no worries
Hey, you should know this
You can't destroy the ones you love...
But you never bothered because you were not mine.

Office Drama

by Ndaba Sibanda

If Mrs. Vithikazi Nhlaba had never considered herself a jealous wife, she certainly made herself a potential target of such accusation after darting into the Human Resource Manager's office only–Good Heavens—to find Miss Simo Mahlangu, the usually calm and shy company secretary, sniggering and posturing below the very nose of Mr. Sinothi Nhlaba.

Long ago, when Mrs. Nhlaba was a young wife, and had verbal bouts and tiffs with Mr. Sinothi Nhlaba, her husband, over his lateness, her rustic aunt once said to her, "Don't raise eyebrows yet. Hold your peace. You're a woman who works hard like an ant bear.

"He can't afford to lose you if he has an ounce of brains in his head. Not maggots or termites. By the same token, you can't seek to kill a snake whilst it's still in its hole, lest there's no snake at all in the first place. Call to mind, our wise elders advised us against holding the flying ant by its head lest it flies off!... and they also said: 'What is horny cannot be hidden (forever). The truth will come out.'"

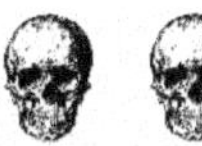

Mrs. Vithikazi Nhlaba respected her aunt, but her head was inundated with countless ideas and unanswered questions. Did her aunt board the bus all the way from eMaguswini to preach such an impossible gospel? "Today, I'm traveling to Bulawayo to tell Vithikazi to be subservient to her husband. I might be rural, old and uneducated, but I know how to handle wayward men." Did she ever give thought to what she was saying? For starters, was it humanly possible and easy not to be suspicious when one partner's concentration had clearly been swayed away? How could her aunt advise her to hold her peace in the face of such a shift? Was that shift not as bad as an act of betrayal? So she was expected to swallow up such nonsense unquestioningly because she worked like an ant bear? What if indeed he had maggots or termites for brains? If her aunt put herself in her shoes for just a few days, would she stand his strange behavior? After all, was she not her maternal aunt? Don't raise eyebrows.

Hold your peace. How can peace be held when wars of disquiet are being waged against one? Was her husband not slipping away from her bit by bit? How could she not raise eyebrows when he was coming home late every night? And as if that were not enough headache on its own, without an explanation or word of greeting he would slump on the couch and sleep soundly? Was his seemingly blissful snoring from the living room not her series of nightmares? Did her aunt have any idea how emotionally disconcerting the whole experience was? How could the unenviable journey of wondering where her husband had been and what he had been up to be an easy or peaceful one?

Hold your peace? Really? What peace? Did her aunt know that she was worried to death about his safety and well-being? For example, what if street thugs pounced on him at night? How would she live with herself and her self-denial? What if he had found omakhwapheni[1] with whom he was spending the better part of the night, and were as usual, feeding him with food spiced with shovels and shovels of their zwanamina[2] in a bid to crown him their boytoy? Hold your peace? Still? Queries and thoughts assailed her mind, her peace, her days and nights. Maybe she was paranoid. Maybe she wanted to be practical. Was it her little cock-eyed illusions and delusions telling her that the man she loved dearly was coming home late night in night out?

When her aunt, who, to her best knowledge had been single since time immemorial, finally left for EMaguswini after a week's stay, Mrs. Nhlaba decided to seek further advice and guidance from a number of diverse spiritual sources.

---

[1] Omakhwapheni: literally meaning "those who hide under the armpits," these are side chicks or secret lovers.
[2] Zwanamina: literally meaning "taste me," these are man-stupefying concoctions.

"Do you know what kind of things dogs eat?" a man in a stuffy and small hut asked.

"I'm looking for a solution to my husband's truancy. Now I'm wondering: What do dogs and what they eat have to do with this problem?" queried Mrs. Nhlaba, trying to suppress a strong wave of impatience.

"Everything. You and I know that it has absolutely everything to do with those domestic animals. Madam. Men are..."

"Oh no, not that antiquated stereotypical stuff about men and dogs!" she found herself interjecting.

"But this is a fact of life, even our elders acknowledged that correlation, that comparison."

"Please, not all men are like that. For example, I've friends, relatives and neighbors whose husbands and boyfriends are consistently loving, faithful and well-behaved. Stop making dangerous comparisons, outdated, outmoded assumptions and conclusions."

"I thought we're talking specifically about your husband's actions, not about the lifestyles and behaviors of your friends, relatives or neighbors. I receive and attend to a lot of people from different walks of life every day. I know what I'm talking about. The last time I checked how most men behaved, the results were the same. Men are..."

The man, wearing some awe-inspiring traditional regalia, was in the process of defending his theory in a defiant, bold and boastful fashion when Mrs. Nhlaba interrupted him. "Look, man, this is the 20th century. Rise from the dead and start to live again. Get a life and wake up. I can clearly see that your view of the modern world is a little dated. It's reeling under a sick, old, parochial and patriarchal ego. You need help because you're a patient languishing from a terrible chronic ignorance. Let me tell you this for free: you've another thing coming if you're entertaining any single idea of ever convincing me that men are nothing else but dogs in disguise. You know what that's called? It's a lame, lousy and loud excuse for lacking true manly qualities. Last week, I wasted my precious money and time funding the trip of my pastoral aunt from EMaguswini all the way to Bulawayo, hoping she would help me deal with my man's delinquency in a mature, fresh and fair manner. Alas, it wasn't to be. Upon arriving, guess what? She categorically told me not to raise eyebrows, but to hold my peace. What audacity. What impetuosity. As if that were not enough, you've seen it fit to waste my cash and time. I've just paid a consultation fee here only to hear you harp on a silly and archaic connection between men and dogs. How does that solve my problem?" She questioned rhetorically as she stormed out of the circular mud-walled, grass-thatched room, whose herbal odor had given her nostrils something to contend with. The traditionalist was startled by Mrs. Nhlaba's unceremonious departure.

Undeterred, she sought the services of fortune tellers and traditional doctors like she was possessed, like they held the key to her happiness. It was as if they held the epicenter of her life and future in their concoctions, in their invocations, in their pronouncements and in their rituals, and even on their horizons and crystal balls.

"What's your husband's favorite food?" asked one female herbalist.

"He relishes isitshwala[3] with okra or isitshwala with beef stew."

"Great! Then I've a panacea to your quagmire."

"What are you going to do?"

"Actually, the remedy lies with what you'll have to do."

"Really?"

"Yes. You should claim your husband back with your hands."

"How, doctor? Follow him like a shadow, and then drag him back home?"

"No. It's simpler than that. Your urine, saliva and lizards' tails will do the trick. You just need to follow the short procedures and prescriptions, and the man will rush back and fall at your feet, begging for forgiveness and love. The die will be cast. Don't you want to be his irresistible queen again?"

"Yes, I do. Mmm ...but my bodily excretions like urine and all ... ngeke bantu[4]!

Honestly, my belief system, my conscience...both don't allow me to..."

"Madam, this is not about your religion. This is about finding a solution to your problem."

Mrs. Nhlaba left in a huff.

One day, one confident and flamboyant prophet gave her what he called his never-failing anointed

---

[3] Isitshwala: a stiff dumpling made from corn or grain.

[4] Ngeke bantu: No way, people.

seawater, and vowed that in the next two days, Sinothi Nhlaba would be back in her warm arms as soon as he had knocked off from work. It was not to be. In the following two days, Mr. Nhlaba bettered his past record of lateness by arriving home after 2:00 a.m. and 3:00 a.m. respectively. Mrs. Nhlaba's anxiety reached boiling points. She would dig into Mr. Nhlaba's pockets and briefcase with the hope of stumbling on some evidence to link it with his sluggishness to be home. There was no mark of feminine touch on his face, no sign of lipstick, except for his lazy eyes that rolled in their sockets each time he arrived.

It soon turned out that Mr. Nhlaba's unpunctuality was none other than the crazy result of his newly-found love—BEER. However, that day when she caught sight of Miss Mahlangu seeking to draw the attention of her husband like a magnet would a drawing pin, her aunt's words speared through her head before disappearing into obsoleteness. She concluded that Miss Mahlangu's intentions were far from being venial. She was a 'devious temptress' playing her devilish cards in a dangerous fashion. Nothing more, nothing less.

As for Miss Mahlangu, she was comfortable and free in her garments. She was of the opinion that a number of rank marshals, drivers and touts were simply nosey, overzealous and judgmental. They had no business in heckling and harassing women over what ladies sported. Did those men have expertise in fashion? They did not look like persons of good taste, either. Far, far from being connoisseurs, at all. Personal hygiene was what they should have been minding. They fooled around as if they had great sensitivity to beauty, civility and culture. What rudeness! Most of them were total strangers to women on the streets. Women doing their business, minding their business. How dare those total strangers to cross a line, to go beyond accepted limits or standards of behavior. Mrs. Nhlaba vowed to put them in their proper place.

In fact, one Monday morning when she was alighting from a city cab, a tipsy emergency taxi tout had remarked, "You're like a twin cab limousine cruising to a palace, girl. Submarine maybe. A loaded bazooka doesn't come any close to this. A top jet-fighter! Yeah!! I've not been to any airport in the world, but I think you fly beyond the furthest clouds, you cruise at 130,000 feet... whatever! Assets is your middle name. If you were sweets, you would be a packet of chocolates. If you were a TV set, you would be that big plasma; I mean a big flat screen. If you were music, you would be an LP, not a 7-single disc. No! And if you were a bed, you would not be a double one. You would be a queen bed! I want to crown you my beautiful big bumblebee baby. My beautiful queen. Tell me, how do I become the king caretaker of that beautiful wealth eh? Please make me rich!"

That morning, Mrs. Nhlaba decided to cough out her anger on the man, "Nx![5] Who are you talking to, hopeless, mannerless drunkard?"

"Obvious, to you big beautiful queen. How can you ask whether the goat is female or male when its back is facing you, baby?"

"Get the hell out of my sight. You must be a mentally

---

[5] Nx!: an expression of disgust or disapproval.

ill dirty daydreamer. A walking dead thing. I'm not your type. Ok? Fuck off, maan[6]! A piece of discarded, smelly and tattered cloth!"

"Take it easy. Easy. You're right 101 percent. I'm sick. I have amatheketheke[7] in my veins, in my body. Once I remove them, and get umvunsankunzi[8] from ikhehla[9] from edladleni[10], I swear I will be grand and back for you. Shame. There will be thunder without rain! Hehehehe, I'm Mr. Mkhonto[11], for your information. That's my nickname. I can sense a beautiful lady from a distance. Suppose you're on the fiftieth floor, coming down in an elevator for queens and beauties and I'm on the first floor, I can tell with my eyes closed that you're landing down, girl. That's me! My heart's hooter is blowing and going: LOVE HELP ME, LOVE HOLD ONTO ME, LOVE FLY WITH MEEE PLEASEEEE!!! I can feel your presence like a good computer detecting a WIFI router. That's me! In fact, I've a special love wireless extender in my body that makes me see you from afar!

'There's a good connection between you and me. Listen to your heart now. Love has no type, no class, no size because it is blind. Did you catch me there? I think you were born for me, and that you're my kind of cow,

---

[6] Maan: a bastardized word used to emphasis something.

[7] Amatheketheke: bodily impurities.

[8] Umvunsankunzi: literally meaning "that which wakes up the bull," this refers to an aphrodisiac, usually a traditional herbal concoction.

[9] Ikhehla: an old man.

[10] Edladleni: a slang term for home or the village.

[11] Mkhonto: a spear.

you know. Don't say I am a piece of tattered cloth. I am helpful. I help drivers and commuters. I am connected.

"You don't know that if you become my queen you will have free rides every day because I know all the kombi drivers here. You will have fresh eggs, cheese, steak, macimbi[12], pies, pizza, ox-tails and tongues of fat cattle, legs and wings of proper chickens from the rural areas and all the choice meat you can dream and think of every day. Not the tasteless chicks you see around here. Maybe you talk like a high class official yet you chew vegetables every day like a rabbit. That will be a thing of the past. I know all the butcher men in the city centre. Let's not talk about my job. Let us talk about our future. Let me oil my engine... Sting. Sting. You will see. Boom! Explosions. Boom! Explosions. Mngci[13]. Mngci..."

Her claim as a fighter for her rights, though not completely immune from street obscenities-- coupled with her dress code was a bold statement about yearning for a certain feminine freedom, dignity and expression. Of course, many a careless and salivating man had used her skimpy dress code as a scapegoat to feel the immensity, elasticity and gentleness of her ample backside. No surprise, then, that she had hurled some unscrupulous men to the courts of law or rained scorching slaps and fists upon them.

When Mrs. Nhlaba unceremoniously walked into

---

[12] Macimbi: mopani worms (considered a delicacy in Zimbabwe and South Africa).

[13] Mngci: a way of swearing.

her husband's office, to her shock and surprise, Miss Mahlangu was strategically bent over a small cabinet file, her sky-blue mini-dress revealing a filmy multicolored undergarment that left little to the imagination. Mr. Nhlaba considered himself as being physiologically normal. No matter how he tried to look away from Miss Mahlangu's backside, he found his rather dizzy glances falling on her, the whole sight playing a game of electricity with his unsuspecting hormones. His body was interiorly battling with a certain tempting chemistry he loved to hate. In SiNdebele, they say eyes are so insatiable they cannot be served with enough food, meaning that even if one told himself to look away from something or someone, more often than not, curious eyes tend to be stubborn and misleading. As hard as he tried to look away, his gaze riveted to Miss Mahlangu when Mrs. Nhlaba lurked about like a cornered snake. Mr. Nhlaba's wife was not prone to being at the centre of various office imbroglios, but she felt obliged to act on what she considered to be her husband's secretary seductive ploy and antics. She had to nip such wayward behavior in the bud, or else she would remain holding to a little feather when the bird had slipped through her clasped hands. The way her husband's eyes seemed to feast on Miss Mahlangu backside made Mrs. Nhlaba insecure and suspicious.

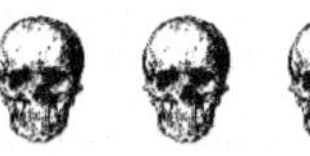

Mrs. Nhlaba used to have a big frame when she was a child. In her twenties, because of the constant hype about the beauty of a slender body promoted and propounded by glossy magazine lifestyle editors and several local and international tabloids, she jumped into a dieting regime. Her daily gym sessions worked wonders as she shed kilos and kilos over a period of six months until she was a lean young beauty. She met her husband Sinothi at the Luveve Gym Trim Centre, who would later shower praises upon her. Then when they started dating, he called her his SSPP, an acronym for Sweet Slender Portable Possession.

"What the heck do you think you're doing, Simo?"

"I'm doing my work?"

"Naked?"

"Your eyes must be deceiving you!"

"Don't be silly, what are you trying to achieve?"

"To meet today's aims and objectives in the most efficient and effective

way."

"Do those aims include showing off your extra-large bums right under the

nose of my husband?"

"I'm doing my work, please respect that."

"Nonsense! Mannerless slut, get your damn lazy ass out of this office!"

"Have you forgotten that I work here, and that I don't report to you? Please

don't push me too far!"

Mr. Nhlaba who had been following the heated exchange of words between the two ladies with interest, suddenly found himself saying, "Please Simo, excuse us." Though his voice had authority, it was devoid of any tinge of harshness or anger. His wife continued to stand in the doorway with her arms crossed over her chest.

Miss Mahlangu looked at him with exaggerated disbelief. She took a cursory look at Mrs. Nhlaba before forcing out a little unhurried cough. As if she were pausing and pondering, she strolled in a wearisome-couldn't-care-less attitude towards her handbag which rested on a small three-legged wooden circular table. She picked it up and then made a leisurely turn. All that acting and dilly-dallying seemed like ages in the eyes and mind of Mrs. Nhlaba. In fact, her blood pressure rose. Her heart seemed to be on the verge of bursting. For a while she was inarticulate with rage. As the drama unfolded, she turned her body into some kind of blockade. She told herself that she would discipline Simo in a way she would not forget for the rest of her life. How could she have the nerve to cat-walk in her husband's august office!

"Vithikazi! Vithikazi! Stop causing a scene here!" bellowed Mr. Nhlaba. He rose unsteadily from his comfortable rocking arm-chair. Like a concerned fireman trying to put out a raging fire, he raced towards the two ladies. They stood there glowering at each other like two world heavyweight boxers sizing up each other before a crucial match. He wedged himself in between them. Mrs. Nhlaba tried to get around him and attempted to land a scathing punch on the oval face of Miss Mahlangu. But her husband took hold of her arm, and pushed her away.

"So you are protecting your girl with oversized bums,

eh?"

"So, this war is about my big backside? Shame on you jealous old woman. Why don't you get your little twin tennis balls surgically boosted? Surgeons can add some flesh!" Miss Mahlangu retorted.

"Shut up, big bitch with gigantic bums!" Vithikazi snapped.

"l thought Bible-carrying grandmamas don't stoop so low as to use such vulgarities!"

"Sinothi, I'll skin your idiotic lady of the night today!" Vithikazi tried pushing her husband out of her way, to no avail.

As Vithikazi was busy seething with anger—Miss Mahlangu sauntered away, for an early lunch break, putting the whole ordeal behind herself. For now.

That night Mrs. Nhlaba lay in bed for what seemed like an eternity, worrying and wondering whether she had overreacted. She asked herself a series of unreciprocated questions. Would she end up her like aunt too? Would she manage to thrust Miss Mahlangu's antics and presence out of her mind and life? Was she in denial? Was she just another jealous wife unable to accept a world sniggering and posturing below *her* own very nose? It was well after 3 a.m when she finally drifted into sleep. She had a dream that transported her to a place of marital bliss, only to wake up in the same abode, aboard a train of disappointed thoughts, doubts and realities.

Obituary to Truth

by Sarah Jane Justice

Truth has been left outside to rot
It begs in empty streets
Flushed raw down rusty gutters
Laced with bleach-stained sighs

Truth dies without a mask
Slapped red with bare-faced scorn
Ripped to fit the shapes of banshees
Who scream against their safety

Truth saved the lives that fight it
Gave strength to hands that rise as fists
Life to feet that drag its name
Breath into the mouths that scorn it

Truth has been painted into lies
Cursed with the shroud of disbelief
The loud declare the death of fact
The selfish lead the blind

Motherhood

by Fable Tethras

The office smelled faintly of mildew and something sweeter that She couldn't quite place. She wished the doctor would open a window or turn on a fan. Anything to help ease the strain on Her senses, but he was too busy poring over Her file to notice the signs of nausea on Her face. She adjusted Herself on the plastic chair and tried to breathe slowly through Her mouth.

"Do you know why you're here?" Dr. Milton had small, rodent-like features highlighted by his thinning hair and unfortunately large ears. He sniffed the air as though something smelled rotten as he leveled his glare at Her.

"Yeah," She said, Her eyes dropping to the threadbare carpet, stained from thousands of feet that had marched across it over the years. She wondered briefly about those feet. Men's, mostly, She was sure. The former prison has been for men and while the former wardens office where She sat now had probably seen a pair or two of women's feet, it probably wasn't many.

"Tell me," he said. He adjusted his necktie and stared at Her over the top of his glasses.

"My father called," She said as She leaned into Her knees. She couldn't breathe in this stuffy office. She wanted to be outside. She wanted to be home, packing for college.

"Yes, but *why* did your father call?"

She pressed Her lids together until the urge to roll Her eyes passed. "Because I'm pregnant."

"Your attitude isn't doing you any favors. We're here to help you." Dr. Milton let out a long-suffering sigh.

Her hands gripped the hard edge of the seat. She focused on a stain on the carpet, just to the right of Dr. Milton's desk. The longer She stared, the more certain She became that it was a dragon, wings outstretched as though trying to fly from it's nylon prison.

Dr. Milton sighed again, but She didn't look up. *If I stare at the dragon, I won't puke. If I stare at the dragon I won't puke.* She thought the words over and over, willing truth into them. "He caught me brewing yarrow tea," She said finally.

"You understand it's illegal for anyone suspected of being pregnant to have yarrow?" Dr. Milton's words were carved in condescension.

"Yeah." She wondered where the dragon would go, if it could escape.

"Well," Dr. Milton said with a sniff, "I can see your father was right to call us. My receptionist should be back shortly with a court order to keep you here until your pregnancy is complete. If you will follow me, I'll have someone show you to your bed."

At first, She couldn't move. This meeting, this joke of an examination, was all the trial She got? No, less than that, She realized. Dr. Milton must have sent his receptionist to get the paperwork before She even arrived.

Dr. Milton sniffed loudly as he opened his door. The rush of fresh air almost felt like salvation to Her. She stood and turned to follow him. Instead, Her knees hit the floor, stomach bile and bits of fruit salad landing just a few feet from the dragon.

The nurse who showed Her to the room offered neither a smile nor a word as they walked down the stark white halls, not even a napkin to wipe the vomit that dribbled from the corners of Her mouth. Posters were hung every few feet. Some with women haloed in sunlight as they smiled down at their distended bellies, others with cherubic children playing or happy families. Each bore a slogan of some sort. "Every child is a gift." "I loved you before you were born." She looked away from the posters and focused on the back of the nurse's head. He had the beginnings of a bald spot there. She wondered if he knew.

The nurse stopped outside a pair of doors with thick glass. On the other side were rows of beds, each set of two were separated by half-walls that were probably supposed to give the illusion of privacy. On the far wall, exactly opposite the doors, was a room surrounded entirely by glass. In it were four nurses who stood rod-straight as they watched the women.

She wasn't prepared for the blast of noise that erupted into the hall when the nurse opened the doors. Moaning, crying, conversation, laughter. Her knees buckled, but the nurse was there, lifting Her upright and pushing Her toward a bed about halfway down the first row. She folded onto it, the metal springs creaking as She did so.

She closed Her eyes as the nurse shuffled off, trying to catch Her breath. She couldn't imagine eight months in this place. Eight months. Eight. Months. By then, She'd be almost nineteen. She'd have to re-apply for college. The scholarships She'd won would be gone. Why had Her father come home early that day?

"Hey." A weight sank onto Her mattress and She looked up. Swirling brown eyes stared back at Her. Their owner was a woman a little older than Her. "I'm Aisha. So you're my new roommate?"

She nodded as Aisha handed Her a tissue.

"How long you got?" Aisha put a hand on Her shoulder and gave a comforting squeeze.

"Eight months," She said as She dabbed at Her mouth. "You?"

Aisha nodded. "I got four months left. Who turned you in?"

"My father." Tears crept down Her cheeks as She thought about him, red-faced, screaming, knocking the teapot from the stove just as it began to whistle.

Aisha sucked air in between her teeth and gave a wide-eyed stare. "That's dirty."

"What about you?" She wasn't sure She really wanted to know, but the conversation gave Her something to focus on.

"My big sister. She can't have kids. Wants this one." Aisha gave a little shrug. "I told her if getting this kid was worth the cost of losing me, she could have it."

It was Her turn to look wide-eyed. "A-are you sick?"

Aisha shook her head and laughed. "No, but I don't have a sister, far as I'm concerned. Nah, I'm healthy." Aisha put her hands on her bulging belly and shook. "Except for this."

She laid Her hand over Her own belly. There wasn't even the hint of a bump yet, but that would change. She let Her eyes crawl across the space She would be sharing with Aisha. The beds were against the outer half-walls. Between them was a six drawer dresser with a mirror. On top of the dresser were several books, neatly lined up and covered with dust. She read the titles: "What to Expect When You're Expecting," "The Girlfriend's Guide to Pregnancy," "Belly Laughs," "Baby Wise," "Childbirth Without Fear."

"Are those yours?" She asked.

She felt the bed shake as a shiver ran through Aisha. "Nah. Those are in every cubicle. We're supposed to read 'em, but almost nobody does."

She stood and paced the little space, keeping Her eyes

trained on the cheap linoleum tiles.

"You giving your baby up for adoption?" Aisha had moved to the center of the bed, her back pressed against the half-wall.

She nodded.

"Someone you know?"

She shook Her head. "My parents said I have to learn to deal with my own mistakes. Closed adoption."

"Look," Aisha said gently, "you and me, we've got it easy. We do our time, hand the baby off to someone happy to have it, and move on with our lives. Not everybody gets so lucky."

She knitted Her eyebrows and looked to where Aisha pointed: a man with a wispy mustache and a belly that looked almost ready to burst. He was sitting on a half-wall on the other side of the room, deep in conversation with two women.

"Max and his husband want the baby. But Max won't dress like a woman, so they put him in here. His husband is fighting to keep the baby once it's born."

She frowned. "They locked him up?"

"All's someone has to do is tell a judge that it's not safe for the baby. They said a pregnant man wasn't safe in society, so here he is."

She watched Max, full of pregnancy glow, for a moment longer before Aisha pointed to a small body, perched on a chair, a copy of "What to Expect When You're Expecting" in her hands and her long black hair hanging like a curtain over her face. "That's Maria. She's twelve."

She let out a long breath. "Are her parents adopting?"

"Foster kid," Aisha said darkly. "And she won't be going back to *that* home."

She stood in the entrance of the cubicle and stared out at the women. So many women.

"Two cubicles over is Tina," Aisha said quietly. "She's six weeks and ectopic. She probably won't make it out of here alive." Aisha paused, letting the words hang in the air. "So yeah, this sucks for you and me, but it's not the end of the world. We get to walk away. Not everyone does."

Her first full day at the birthing center began at seven the next morning. She stood behind Aisha in a line of women who were marched silently from the sleeping area to the cafeteria, and made to stand against a wall as they slowly worked their way toward the long metal tables that held their breakfast. The tables were organized by food type, and behind each station stood a nurse who checked each woman's name against a list.

"You get three pieces of fruit, a bowl of oatmeal, toast with peanut butter, and a glass of milk today," a nurse who looked more like a drill sergeant told Her.

She opened Her mouth to protest, but Aisha gave Her a little poke to the ribs and shook her head. She closed Her mouth and followed Aisha from station to station, collecting Her allotted items

"Everybody, this is the newest hostage," Aisha said as

she plopped into one of the two empty seats at the end of the long table that looked like it belonged in a public school. Aisha pointed to each person, muttered a name and moved to the next.

Four pairs of eyes turned toward Her as She sat next to Aisha, Her hands trembling a little. "Hi," She said quietly.

"You look like you're in for a long stay," said the one Aisha had called Max the day before. He wore the same shapeless medical gown as everyone else, but had tied it on backward and pinned much of the bottom shut.

She nodded and swirled Her spoon in Her oatmeal.

"Me too. Seven months left on my sentence," said a woman with hair that had once been dyed blue or green, and whose name started with an N. Nancy? Nadine? Noreen? She couldn't remember.

"She doesn't talk much," Aisha said. "So Max, how's the case going?"

Max shook his head and stabbed a strawberry with his fork. "When I get out of here, we're moving to the West."

The group let out a collective gasp.

"Shhh! Don't let them hear you," the N-named woman said.

Max laughed. "Why? Because they might try to make my life hard?"

"Don't matter," said the woman with red hair—Kelsey or Kelly, maybe. "I heard they aren't letting anyone else in."

"They're always saying that," Max said. "It's just

propaganda."

She closed Her eyes and imagined the West. A crescent-shaped haven for people who wanted freedom of choice. The last three states that still allowed abortion.

When She was seventeen, She had gone over there with some friends for a concert. The wall that blocked off the West from the rest of the US was a steel and concrete monstrosity topped with barbed-wire and surrounded by officers from the Happy Families Department.

She and Her friends had waited hours, showing forged permission slips from their parents, and waiting for the results from the mandatory blood test that proved they weren't pregnant, but crossing through the barrier had been like entering a dream world. Free healthcare, freedom to marry, living wages, equality, and, of course, freedom of choice.

They had only been there for a day, but She remembered every detail. When She had come home, only two of their original group of five had come with Her.

"You have to finish before prenatal yoga, or they'll give you a feeding tube," Aisha said, pulling Her from the memory.

She looked down at the plate and frowned. She was the only one who hadn't finished yet. She shoveled the food into Her mouth and walked from the cafeteria with squirrel cheeks as everyone filed into a barbwire-enclosed yard for prenatal yoga.

"We need to tell you the rules," Aisha said as they

stretched on ragged mats.

"Consider this your orientation," the one with a K-name said.

"First," the N-named one said, holding up her index finger, "you have to clear your plate at every meal."

"Second, don't skip any of your classes. Even if you're tired or sick. The instructors decide what to do, not you," Aisha said.

"Third, don't talk about what's happening on the outside or about the W-E-S-T," Max said. "This girl Lola, couldn't have been more than fifteen, she started giving everyone updates about the outside, next day, she was gone."

"Gone?" She arched an eyebrow.

"Breaking the rules gets you put on bed rest." Aisha shivered. "They strap you to a bed in a private room and keep you there until you deliver."

She swallowed Her horror and took a deep breath. "Okay, so what are the rest of the rules?"

"It's easier if you think of it this way: do nothing to draw attention to yourself. Be a robot until you leave," the K-named one said.

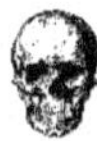  

"You have a visitor," Dr. Milton said.

The smell was worse today, but She had mastered the art of shallow breathing through Her mouth.

"Who?" She looked around the small room, as though this unexpected guest could be hiding in a corner. In the five weeks She'd lived in this place, no one had visited.

No one had even bothered to call. She wasn't sure if any of Her friends knew what had happened, but Her parents certainly did. Yet they'd maintained radio silence.

Dr. Milton grinned, stood, and opened the door. Beyond it waited Robert, who smiled nervously at Her. He wiped a loose strand of limp, straw-colored hair from his forehead and sat in the plastic seat next to Hers, but kept his eyes trained on the wall behind Dr. Milton's desk.

She studied him as he ignored Her. His wiry frame was pulled inward, and his knee was rocking from side-to-side. Whatever he'd come for, She knew it wasn't good news.

"I believe you two have something to discuss," Dr. Milton said as he lowered himself into the leather chair behind his desk.

"Uh. Yeah." Robert nodded and turned toward Her, taking Her hand. "So, right. Um. Sweetie, I have bad news. I want you to know I love you, and we'll get through this together, but I can't sign off on adoption."

The world seemed to drop away from Her. "What?"

"Look. I mean," he paused and itched at his arm, "my parents. They can't take the baby, because they're health isn't great, but, um, they said they'd pay for my college, right through a PhD, if I didn't give up their grandkid."

"Oh god, I think I put the condom on wrong. Whatever you want to do, babe," She said in a voice that mimicked his. "You got me the yarrow!"

Suddenly, She could smell his sweat on Her body, feel

his hands on Her breasts, his lips on Her neck as he begged. *I want to be inside you.* He'd told Her. *We'll be careful. I need you so bad.* Why She'd ever said yes would be a question that haunted Her for the rest of Her life. Maybe it was hormones, or the thrill of prom, whatever it was, it had been a stupid decision.

"I didn't have grades like yours," he said defensively, "I can't go to school without help. And it's not like it'll be all on you. I'm going to visit the baby and take her on weekends and stuff during school breaks. And there's child support? That'll help, right? I just made a payment today, so you'll owe this place less when you get out."

It took Her a moment to realize the roar She heard was not the carpet dragon coming to life, but the sound of Her blood rushing in Her ears. She pulled Her hand from his and watched it shake with a rage She couldn't express. "I hate you," She whispered.

"Now, now. Robert's doing his part. He's taking on financial responsibility, and he's committing to visitation even while going to school. I'd say that's commendable." Dr. Milton rewarded Robert with a pride-filled smile.

"I don't want to keep it," She said flatly, pointing a finger at Her ever-growing belly. "Either you take full custody or it goes up for adoption."

Robert put his hands in front of him, palms out. "I can't. I wish I could, but I can't. I can't take care of a baby full-time and I need the money from my parents. This is the only way."

She glared at him, anger rolling off of Her in waves. "The only way is for you to condemn me for doing what *you* wanted."

Dr. Milton walked to the door and opened it. "I think this might be enough for the day, Robert. I think she needs some time to process, but I'm sure she'll be happy with this arrangement soon enough."

Robert stood up so fast his plastic chair toppled to the side. He jumped and offered Her a guilty look before bolting through the door. She stood to leave as well, but Dr. Milton closed the door again and resumed his seat. "I'm very concerned about your reaction."

She blinked mutely. He stared back for a moment, then leafed through the papers on his desk. She lowered Her gaze to stare at the dragon. "I don't want kids," She whispered.

His beady eyes narrowed. "If you didn't want kids, you shouldn't have had sex."

"You've never had sex for pleasure? What? Every man only does it to make a baby?" She couldn't stop Herself from jumping to Her feet, screaming.

"It's different for men. We aren't vessel's for life." He grinned at Her outburst and leaned back in his chair. "Now sit down, or I'll be forced to put you on bed rest."

Her jaw opened and closed for a moment. She counted to five, then sat again.

"Now, all mothers who choose to keep their babies must attend classes during their stay here," he said, holding out a single sheet of paper. "Usually each mother chooses her own classes, but given the circumstance, I've gone ahead and picked yours for you."

She stared at the dragon, unmoving. "What about mothers who don't choose to keep it?"

"What does that matter? You've chosen to keep yours." He sounded genuinely bewildered.

"I didn't choose. I'm being forced."

Dr. Milton twitched his rat lips and sighed. "Call it whatever you like, but you'll be raising a child so you'll be taking these classes." He flicked the paper from his fingers and watched as it wafted over his desk and onto Her lap.

"Tina ruptured while you were gone," Aisha said as soon as she returned. Aisha was pacing the room, softly humming to herself. "Won't know if she survived, of course. I hope she did."

She nodded and stood mute in front of Aisha, the class list in Her hand.

"What's that?"

She wasn't sure if She should tell Aisha. Tina might be dead, suddenly having to keep the baby seemed like such a little thing to be upset about. What was eighteen years compared to a life sentence?

Aisha reached out and tugged the list from Her hand, her eyes growing wider as she read.

"Baby Basics, Teaching Toddlers, Healthy Cooking, Maintaining a Clean Home...They really nailed you." Aisha handed the list back in disgust.

She only nodded.

"So you decided to keep the baby? Congratulations."

Her jaw worked, but no words came out, so She shook Her head.

Aisha's features positioned themselves into a look of pure confusion. "You didn't choose to keep the baby?"

She nodded.

"But they're making you take parenting classes?"

She nodded.

"Give me something here."

"He won't give up his rights. He's making me keep it." Tears poured from Her eyes. She felt Aisha's soft arms wrap around Her as She sank to the ground. The torrent kept coming. Her body shook with the flood, desperate moans escaped from Her lips.

Aisha rocked Her slowly, whispering gentle words as it wore on. More arms and more words surrounded Her as Her rage dripped onto the floor.

"What'd they do this time?" She wasn't sure who was asking.

"They're making her keep the baby," Aisha supplied. There was a chorus of What!? and How!?

"The Father's Rights Protection Act?" That, She knew, was Max's voice. Aisha must've nodded. "We tried using that, but I guess it only applies to heteros." There was such misery in Max's voice, more tears poured out of Her. He was due any day now, but his husband had lost the case two weeks ago. Max was giving birth to someone else's child now.

"I'd give you mine, if I could," She whispered.

"When you get out of here, come find us in the West,

and we'll see what we can do." As he spoke, She heard his voice crack. She focused on the world around Her and realized She wasn't nearly the only one crying.

She was exhausted when She sat down for dinner. Their group had shrunk to three. Kelsey had gone into labor only days after Max, and Aisha and Nina weren't interested in making any new friends.

She looked down at Her plate of chicken and spinach and swallowed the urge to vomit. At fifteen weeks, everything smelled too strong. Nothing looked appetizing, but Her OBGYN, an elderly woman with graying hair and a sympathetic smile, had assigned a meal plan nonetheless.

"So what did you learn today?" Nina asked in her best teacher voice.

She ticked off each item on Her fingers. "Proper care and maintenance of cloth diapers, the proper way to teach colors, the importance of the food pyramid, and how to fold fitted sheets."

"So what is the proper way to teach colors?" Nina grinned and took a bite of her salad.

"Repetition," She sighed. "Same as teaching numbers, the alphabet, shapes."

"Wow. Clearly no one would ever figure that out on their own." Nina rubbed her fingers through her hair and glared around the room.

"It's almost the same thing every lesson, just a different topic. I guess that's how they stretch it out though." She cautiously chewed some spinach, washing it down with a sip of water.

"I would've represented you, you know." Nina reached a hand out and lightly brushed the top of Hers. Nina had been a lawyer before being locked up. She'd been an active voice against the bans and the internments. Nina also suspected her husband of intentionally breaking the condom.

"Don't let them hear you," Aisha said into her plate. "You know they want you on bed rest."

Nina grinned and waved her fork around the room, the nurses at each entrance, the ones manning the food lines, the ones walking among the tables. "It's not bed rest I'm worried about."

"Still trying for an accident?" Aisha eyed the cameras as she spoke. Those blinking red eyes were the only real concession on the law that demanded millions remained locked up during their pregnancy. The cameras recorded twenty-four hours a day and were monitored by a team from the ACLU to ensure the almost completely male staff, namely the nurses, did not lay an inappropriate finger on any confined person. That didn't stop the nurses from trying to arrange accidents for those they disliked the most, though.

"One bad fall, and I'm a murderer," Nina said.

"So don't give them more reasons," Aisha said warningly.

She speared more spinach and stuffed it into Her mouth, then followed it with a piece of chicken as another wave of nausea rolled over Her.

Without Aisha's light snores for company, She felt, for the first time since She'd come to this mad place, entirely alone. Aisha's bed had been stripped, and her few personal items removed that morning, only hours after her water broke.

She had seen plenty of women go into labor, but witnessing Her larger-than-life roommate moan in primal pain while the nurses took their time strapping her into a gurney had been different. Aisha had been so pale, caked with sweat and fear. It left Her shivering with a cold that came from the center of Her chest.

She lay in bed, listening to the symphony of the others in the dark. Muffled sobs, muttering, shifting on the stiff mattresses. Plenty were snoring, but none of them with the same gentle cadence Aisha had. She wished She knew if Her friend was okay, but She knew the nurses would give nothing more than a sneer if She asked.

A new roommate would probably arrive the next day. From what She heard, there were dozens in county jails around the state waiting for a bed here. Christa, who had come a few weeks earlier, had told them congress was now issuing rewards to people who turned in anyone pregnant who could be a danger to the fetus. Lula had also told them textbooks were removing all instances of the words "zygote," "embryo," and "fetus" in favor of "baby." The nurses had halted the conversation and taken

Lula to bed rest.

She rolled onto Her side and tried in vain to get comfortable. Her back ached and She longed for an extra pillow, but there was a one pillow, one blanket policy.

She closed Her eyes and thought about the dragon in the doctor's office. She had decided the aged brown carpet was hiding the dragon's true color. When it emerged from its prison, it would be sapphire blue, with eyes the color of violets. It wouldn't breathe fire, but ice. It would imprison anyone who tried to stop them as they journeyed to the West. Once there, She'd decided they would seek out Max and his husband. If they still wanted the baby, it would be all theirs. She would apply to colleges and go to whichever would take Her. She'd earn Her fine arts degree and become a photographer.

In Her spare time, She'd work with one of the resistance groups She'd heard about. The ones who helped pregnant women sneak through the wall. She would meet new people and create a new family that who would never dream of sending Her to a place like this.

She fell asleep with a smile on Her face.

"This will be a bit cold," Dr. Lopez said with a smile.

She nodded and felt Her muscles tighten as the cold gel touched Her skin. With a gloved hand, Dr. Lopez moved the transducer against Her belly. She tried to focus on the yellow walls or even the sterile counter of the examination room, but Her eyes kept trailing back to the black and green screen where a tiny thing kicked and wiggled.

"Your daughter looks completely healthy," Dr. Lopez said a few minutes later.

A daughter. A baby girl. She squeezed Her eyes shut and nodded.

"I'm worried about you though." Dr. Lopez spoke in an obviously faked casual tone. "The baby looks great, but you haven't really gained enough weight, and it looks like maybe your hair is starting to fall out. Is there anything you'd like to talk about?"

She shrugged and looked at the monitor again. A girl. *I'm getting you to the West,* She said silently.

"I know you've decided to keep the baby. Are you maybe having some first-time mom jitters? Or maybe reconsidering the possibility of adoption?"

"Father's Rights Protection Act," She said, still staring at the screen. A daughter.

Dr. Lopez flipped off the screen and set the transducer next to it. "You wanted an adoption?"

She nodded.

Dr. Lopez sat on her stool and peered into Her eyes. "Tell me how you're feeling," she said softly.

She narrowed Her eyes and pressed Her lips together.

"Like all OBs, I'm obligated to assist with any and all pregnancies brought to me from a Give Life A Chance facility, but I don't work for them. Everything you say here is confidential. I won't tell anyone what you say, but I need to know what's going on to be able to help you."

"I'm depressed," She said before She could stop

Herself. "I'm angry. I'm scared. I feel trapped. I don't want kids."

Dr. Lopez nodded and squinted her brown eyes. "Under normal circumstances, I'd prescribe you a light anti-depressant, but I'm not allowed. I'm going to increase your vitamin C and B and recommend more exercise." Dr. Lopez reached out a gloved hand and squeezed Her shoulder.

"So what'd the doc say?"

She looked at Her roommate as She flopped on the bed. The fifty-two year old had a way of speaking that made Her think of a cocktail waitress in a nightclub. "I'm having a girl."

"I'm so sorry." Lucinda shook her head and tsked. "At least it's not much longer."

She nodded and pulled the pillow over Her face. She wished She could say more, but the nurse who walked Her back to Her cubicle hovered in the doorway, pretending to survey the room.

"Got four girls, myself," Lucinda said as she reached down and touched her toes. "If this one's the same, it'll at least even me out. Want a boy though, fewer complications for him."

She started to nod, then realized the pillow was over Her face and gave a thumb's up instead. Tears were beginning to prickle the corners of Her eyes, and while She didn't care if Lucinda saw, She wasn't about to let the nurses know. A little girl. How could She bring a little girl into this world? It seemed cruel. It seemed reckless.

She slid Her hands under the pillow and pressed them against Her eyelids. *The dragon,* She thought to Herself. *Think of the dragon.* She imagined flying on it's back, high above the wall. Her arms were wrapped around a girl of about three. The girl was laughing as they made their descent, a handful of flower petals gripped in her tiny fist.

The walk to Dr. Milton's office was taking longer with each trip. With only four weeks left on Her estimated date of confinement, Her body had taken on a size and shape that felt foreign to Her.

The nurse was a good ten feet ahead of Her before he noticed how far behind She'd fallen. He marched to Her and hooked a hand on Her elbow, pulled Her through the maze to Dr. Milton's office. She stumbled through, barely keeping pace and panting at the exertion by the time they made it to the door.

At first, She could only stare. The walls were blue as a robin's egg. The plastic chairs had been replaced with cushioned ones. Even the desk, which had been gleaming and beautiful, had been replaced. Worst of all, the carpet had gone in favor of black and white tile. The dragon had escaped without Her.

"It's a shock, I know," said Dr. Milton. "But please come in. Shut the door behind you."

She stepped onto the unfamiliar tile and placed

Herself in the unfamiliar chair. Their customary staring contest ended with Dr. Milton's sigh.

"You have a couple of guests today, so we're going to head into my conference room," he said as soon as She was comfortable.

She glared at him and struggled to Her feet. They walked back the way She had come, a full fifty yards before Dr. Milton threw open an unmarked door to the left. He walked in and seated himself at the long dark table, but She stood stiff at the threshold, taking in the room. It's pinkish walls, the wide windows that stood opposite, letting in the weak January sunlight, the blue carpet that was far more plush than anything She'd walked on in a long time.

Eyes turned to Her as She stood there. Dr. Milton's, Her mother's, Her father's, Robert's. She could smell a trap, but could do nothing to stop it. She walked in slowly and sat at the head of the table, opposite Dr. Milton, ignoring the chair Robert pulled out next to him. She took Her time, adjusting the standard-issue hospital gown, pulling up the white socks that covered Her otherwise bare feet, brushing the lank strands of hair from Her face. Finally She looked at them, one by one. Her father's face was almost as red as his flannel shirt, his thick fingers thumping rhythmically on the table. Her mother had been to a salon recently, probably that morning. Her hair was a blond that didn't come naturally and her skin had a faint glow. Robert looked almost the same as when She'd seen him months ago, though he'd cut his hair short and seemed to have given up the torn jeans look. He was dripping with sweat, nervous about something.

"Is it Christmas already?" She asked.

The other three squirmed in their seats. Dr. Milton let out a long sigh.

"Sorry," She said in a tone dripping with sarcasm, "I forgot. Must be that pregnancy brain everyone talks about."

Her mother let out a little sob and squeezed Her father's hand. Robert's eyes slid to the table.

"So what? Did someone die?" She leaned back in the chair, savoring the cushioned seat. It's softness felt like a luxury.

"Robert?" Her father's voice sounded more like a command than a question.

"Right. Yeah. So," he twisted in his seat, finally looking at Her, "I know you said no before, but, I, well, uh, will you marry me?"

She opened Her mouth, but he held up a hand as he fumbled in his pocket. In a move that looked more like falling that squatting, he dropped onto one knee and produced a ring. She squinted at it's familiar shape, then shifted Her eyes to Her mother's hand, where only a gold wedding band resided.

"You borrowed my mother's engagement ring?"

Her mother let out a sharp gasp and her father cleared his throat.

"Yeah. I'll buy you your own, I promise. I'm working full-time at Budsy's, so it shouldn't take too long." He had the decency to turn a deep plum shade.

The hairs on the back of Her neck prickled to attention. "How are you managing college and a full-time job?"

His arm dropped to his side, and his body sagged closer to the floor. He moved like he was about to stand, but thought better of it and only switched knees. "I dropped out of school. College is, well, it's really hard. Harder than I thought. It's just, it's not for me."

"Then sign the papers," She said.

"I can't. My parents are letting me live with them until I can afford my own place—letting *us* live with them. The three of us. As a family..."

"If you say no, your parents have agreed to pay for your first month in single parent housing. We have, of course, a list of approved jobs for people in your...situation, but I must warn you, the job market doesn't look kindly on unwed mothers." The chair beneath Dr. Milton squeaked as he leaned forward and licked his lips.

"Just do the right thing. Please." It was the first words Her mother had spoken to Her in almost a year, and she couldn't be bothered to meet Her eyes.

Slowly, She looked at each of them. Her mother, Her father, Dr. Milton, and Robert, still on his knee. She pursed Her lips and spat in his face.

Bed rest wasn't as bad as She thought it might be. The

straps on Her wrists and ankles itched, and the catheter scraped, but the feeding tube and IV meant She could simply lie there, letting all the work of living be done for Her. Twice a day, two nurses came to change bags and exercise Her arms and legs, and Dr. Lopez came to see Her twice a week. Otherwise, She just had to exist.

She had been indignant at first. Robert had given Her much more damaging fluids, but he'd received no punishment. Now though, She spent Her time plotting. She would move into the apartment, care for the baby and entertain the friends and relatives who would come by to goggle. She'd tolerate Robert's presence, and smile sweetly at his parents. Then, when the visitors stopped, around week three She guessed, She'd take a bus to Reno. The twelve hour ride wouldn't leave time for much suspicion, and, hopefully, She'd have a contact who could help smuggle Her across the border. There, She'd reunite Max and his husband with the baby and be on Her way. It wasn't a perfect plan, She knew, but it was the best She could do under the circumstances.

She had been in agony for almost three hours by the time a nurse responded to Her screams. His stony face drained of color as soon as he looked at Her, cementing the suspicion She already had: something was wrong.

She couldn't count the number of nurses who pushed Her bed down the hall and into the delivery room. They moved in and out of Her vision as She struggled to stay conscious. Suddenly, Her wrists were free and someone was forcing Her upright.

"We're just giving you some medication," Dr. Lopez called from beneath a set of blue scrubs. "We need to do a c-section to help the baby."

The minutes were hours as the epidural worked its way into Her bloodstream, but soon She was on Her back, listening to sounds that should have been words, but were not. A blue partition separated Her from the lower half of Her body. She looked around for some comfort, but a single glowing spotlight was Her only companion. She closed Her eyes and focused on the dragon. She might not be riding its sapphire back to the West, but She could still find it here, in this sterile room.

When She opened Her eyes again, She was alone. The partition was gone and a blanket covered Her. She lifted a hand and gazed at it, struggling to understand that She wasn't strapped down any longer. Finally, She understood. There was a baby now. They no longer needed to imprison Her. She tried to sit up, but the world spun in resistance, and She lay back down again. Muffled voices could be heard on the other side of the room. An argument, She thought. The doors burst open, and Dr. Lopez strode into the room. Behind her were two nurses who angrily looked on as the door swung shut in their faces.

"Please help me," She said weakly. "Please. I need to get my daughter West. Do you know anyone? Please?" She had intended to be more strategic, more cautious, but the words fell out of her before She could stop them.

Dr. Lopez wheeled a stool next to Her bed and stroked sweat-slick hair from Her face. Dr. Lopez's face was puffy and pale. "Listen carefully, we don't have long. Some time between our last appointment and this morning, the baby turned sideways."

She went very still, staring into the doctor's glistening eyes.

"The baby couldn't get out. Under normal circumstances, we would perform an emergency Cesarean section and everything would be fine. But the nurses say you didn't make a sound for the three hours before they brought you here." Dr. Lopez rolled her eyes as she spoke, making it clear what she thought of the nurses' story.

She squinted her eyes, still not comprehending.

"The baby didn't make it. Dr. Milton is already filing murder charges. He's going to have your records unsealed, he'll say you were depressed, that you didn't want the baby, and that you intentionally kept your labor secret so the baby would die."

A gurgling sound escaped Her lips. The baby was gone, but She still wasn't free.

"You have two options, spend the rest of your life in jail-" The doors burst open again, this time the nurses were flanked by two officers. Dr. Lopez grabbed Her hand and squeezed, then followed the officers from the room.

The world darkened around Her. They were going to arrest Her. The baby was dead. The baby was dead and they were going to arrest Her. Dr. Lopez said she had two options. Go to jail or...what? She balled Her hands into fists and felt something dig into the flesh of Her palm. She opened the hand Dr. Lopez had held.

It was an empty syringe. She stared at it. Why had Dr. Lopez left it? Was it an accident? The monitor beeped to Her left. She jumped and turned. She stared as the number for Her pulse rose beyond the IV tubes that hung from a hook behind Her bed. She stared at the syringe again and finally understood. She sat up, ignoring the spinning world, and willed Her shaking fingers to pull the syringe's plunger as far as it would go. Carefully, carefully, She screwed it into the IV tube.

If She couldn't go West, She'd go south.

Collection

by Joann Renee Boswell

how long have I left you
sitting there, plentiful dust
like so many Sunday morning
mega church congregants?

you are a nine-car pileup
I-5 traffic instigator,
precious debris s c a t t e r e d :
quarter portions of donated

day-old pastries, folded programs
like fans, pencil shards, felt Jesus
and donkeys lounging on plastic
palm fronds, nilla wafers, tiny stacks

teetering purple-tinged communion cups,
buckets of red licorice and severed
Foosball players, red letters s p l a y e d

o p e n for pap smear annual exam —

all smug before, *now* you c o w e r
back row garaged bookshelf.
each a time capsule *twerking*
(as modestly as possible),

eager as history to revive my memories.
these B - I - B - L - Eees haunt me:
pink patent leather Precious Moments,
prized first, pairs well with saddle shoes.

splatter-paint teen study Bible, fortune
taped on cover: "happy news is on its way to you".
grandpa's navy blue King James, just one
verse highlighted, "You cannot serve both God and
money."

The Message, silicon green, smells
like my little ponies. handful of Gideon's
take themselves too seriously
(multiplying myth / history hybrid-bunnies).

two red show-offs, golden
edging and engraved for me,
the insides crowded like diaries
(bubble lettering: testament

to two-year discipleship intensive).

and still more, silver and cerulean, unremarkable
reminders conflating nostalgia with worth.
too much collateral damage,   and y e t

the people packed in your pages still
hold promise. sacred interactions,
precious friendships. I can't stomach
throwing you out with the holy water.

I l i n g e r in the wreckage,
sifting what's salvageable —
Easter pageant pre-dawn preparations,
a donut and community.

Lost Island Story Hour

by Eric Witchey

I tell myself I'm not hiding. I just don't want to disturb the old man's reading. He still believes reading can change the world.

I should knock him out with a coconut and carry him to the raft. I owe him at least that. I take a deep breath. The tide's out. The sun's high. Decay and sea salt lace the air.

Just above tide-line, in the shadows of mangroves and thorn thickets, the white sand is still cool on my calloused feet. I crouch low behind the bole of a coconut palm and grind my bare feet deep into the sand.

He's not so different from when I was a kid. Certainly, the palm trees and white sands are not the library's terrazzo, walnut, and brass; but his impish smile and loud guffaw are the same.

He has stones and driftwood logs arranged in a circle. I know that in his mind children sit on those seats in rapt attention. The Saturday afternoon children's readings were always important to him. Back in the world, even in the face of short-sighted cutbacks, low staffing, home web surfing, and pressure from the mayor to close the library, he kept the reading circles going.

Shaded by the tattered blue tarp I hung between two palms for him, he peers over his half glasses. The lenses were lost over a year ago. The gold-plated frames have salt-air corrosion in the scratch marks along the ear-pieces.

I feel guilty about his glasses. I broke the first lens when I hit him. That was when I still thought he was sane -- when I thought he was just pretending he believed we still lived in Ohio.

He pauses in his reading. He turns the book outward so his audience can see the pictures.

There are no pictures. He can't see the words on the pages. It doesn't matter. We only have one book, a Polynesian cookbook that washed up three years ago. Even if his glasses worked, he couldn't read whatever language it's in.

He recites the stories by heart. They're the same tales he read to me when I was a child.

I listen. The emphasis is the same. The rising gray and black eyebrows are the same, perhaps a little more salt than pepper now. The only real difference is the long gray and black ponytail over his shoulder. Now and then, he touches it, tugs it a little. I wonder how that would have gone over in Ohio -- that long-haired, crazed librarian look.

He puts the book in his lap and closes it gently. "That

is all we have time for today," he says. His voice is steady. His diction precise -- proud.

His pocket watch stopped a long time ago. My digital still hums away on its little lithium cell. I imagine that will eventually run down, but I glance at it. Three o'clock. Somehow he knows, right down to the second, when it's time for the kids to meet their parents at the front of the library.

He spreads his arms to take in the imagined hugs and snuggles. Rising, he makes as if to shepherd the kids to the doors. Barefoot thru the sand, he herds the ghost children of his past.

I can't help wondering if my face is worn by one of his ghosts. Part of me hopes so.

Not my face now. Not the brown, weather-hardened face of my thirty-eight year-old manhood. I wouldn't wish that on him. Better that he sees the round, corpulent wonder-filled face of my early years, the years before the trouble in my family, before he took me in as a foster child.

He closes an imaginary door, puts his hands on the small of his back, and stretches. The gesture is as old as he is, I'm sure. I remember it from every session of every Saturday of every summer of my life before college.

He turns.

I sigh along with him. We have long ago synchronized our sighs in this weekly ritual of his insanity. His sigh is one of regret that the children are gone for another week. Mine is one of nostalgia, of fear, of release from this overt manifestation of his insanity.

"Mr. Morton," I say. I step away from the brush.

He starts. Then he smiles and peers over his glasses.

I know immediately that he isn't seeing the man in front of him. When he sees me as I am, he looks through the empty frames. When he sees me as I was, he looks over the tops.

"Little William," he says. "Hiding in the stacks? You should be meeting your mother."

I've given up trying to get him to understand his life here. Instead, I play along. "I needed to check these books, Mr. Morton."

He nods and grins. "What do you have this week? More adventures? Science Fiction? Fantasy? The next in the Gormenghast trilogy?"

I step out of the palm shadows. The rainbow streak of a running lizard skips over my foot and disappears into the thicket. In the sun, the white sand warms my calluses. I offer up my empty hands as if I'm holding several volumes. "Kontiki," I say.

"Thor Heyerdahl."

"I'm building a raft," I say.

"From reeds? To sail the Pacific?"

"Sort of," I say. "I'm using coconuts."

He guffaws. "You are one of my very favorites, William," he says. "And where do you propose to find enough coconuts to float you across the Pacific?"

I look at his feet. There are three coconuts near enough for him to kick. "I've been collecting them," I say. "I get them at the grocery. I've almost got enough."

He realizes I'm serious; or, he realizes the child he sees is serious. He raises a bushy eyebrow. Rather than burst my bubble, he changes the subject.

I almost cry at his kindness even though it's thoroughly demented.

"What else do you have there?" he asks.

"Single Line Fishing in Deep Water," I say.

"Like Santiago?" He reaches out to take my invisible books. I hand them to him.

"Who?"

"Santiago," he repeats. He turns away and heads toward an imaginary counter where the checkout stand should be. I mean, where it would be. He paces off the distance perfectly. My childhood memory knows his gait, the number of steps, the position he'll take, an elbow on the counter, one hand moving books through a scanner, his eyes on me while he continues to chat about my books.

"The Old Man And the Sea," he says. "A great book. With your love of adventure, I think, William, that you would enjoy it. Shall I get our copy for you? I'm sure it has been checked in."

Of course, I know the book. I just didn't remember the name of the old man.

Santiago.

I remember now. What was the boy's name? It doesn't matter. "I think I've got enough for this week," I say.

"I'm surprised," he says. "Only two. You usually leave

with a whole armload."

"Building a raft takes a lot of time," I say. "I don't have any help."

He hands me the imaginary volumes. He nods, smiles, and peers over his frames.

He has to look up at me to peer over the frames. Funny how that look makes me feel small, like I'm still a child standing in front of the tall, kindly librarian that took me in. I want to please him somehow. I want to help him. I remind myself that I'm trying to save his life.

"Maybe," I say, "you could help me with the raft?"

"I have never built a raft, William."

"But I bet you've read all about them."

He smiles. "Reading and doing are not the same."

I smile and speak one of his pet mantras to him. He must have said it to me a thousand, thousand times while I was growing up. "Begin to learn a thing by reading. Make it yours by doing."

He tosses his pony tail over his shoulder and throws back his head and laughs. He shakes so hard he has to hold his glasses to his head. In spite of my fear for him, I smile. He might be insane, but his humor's intact. We laugh together.

"I'll help if I can," he says. "Under one condition."

"What?" I ask.

"You have to come to next Saturday's reading hour. Two-o'clock sharp," he says.

I hope we're both off the island by then. Even so, I agree.

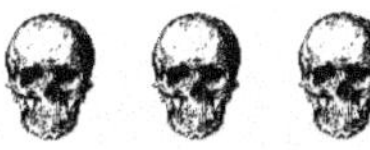

"What we need are some good planks," he says.

I stand up from untying the knotted edges of nylon netting I found hung up on the basalt ridge at the North end of the island. There's enough netting to make maybe ten large bags of coconuts. Hell, Papillon escaped Devil's Island on one. With ten, we can support a platform, a lean-to, an outrigger, and a sail.

I've already finished the platform and outrigger. They float well enough without the coconuts, but the coconuts will let us load the platform and stay high and dry -- I hope.

"Why planks?" I ask.

"To make the story work. There is always a good shipwreck and planks and part of a boat."

"Always?"

"Well, not in Ohio," he says. "But in Gulliver. In Robinson Crusoe. In Dynotopia."

I laugh. He laughs.

"Grass lines do not hold up well in salt water," he says.

I nod. I continue to work on the nylon netting. "We'll test it on fresh water. On Ganges Pond," I say. This seems to please him. "Proof of concept," I say.

He puts down the blue plastic tarps, the sail he's lashing together. Peering over his glasses, he smiles and squints one eye. "Sometimes," he says, "I think you are a lot older in your head than you are in your body, William. Your reading will serve you well as an adult. When you grow up, you can come and write grants for me at the Library."

"I'd like that," I say. I don't remind him that we wouldn't be here if one of my grants hadn't come through. It was for him. It was supposed to help him. It was his dream to SCUBA uncharted Islands in the South Pacific. He wanted to do a coffee table book -- underwater pictures, big plates of pretty fish and corals, a message to the world to save the oceans.

I hadn't expected the grant to come through. None of the others had. The library was dying. His heart was dying with it. At the time, I laughed and thanked God for the gift that might save him.

If that grant hadn't come through, we wouldn't have been on the SCUBA charter when it went down. We wouldn't have had to bury Captain Andy.

I wipe warm salt water from my eyes.

"I think I had better go," he says. "I am quite sure your mother will want to feed you soon, and I have a date with Santiago tonight."

I want him to keep working, to not go off into the jungle and pretend he has a home, an easy chair, a floor lamp, and a copy of The Old Man and the Sea.

"We're almost done," I say.

"Gange's Pond will keep. Remember your promise," he says. "Tomorrow is Saturday."

"I'll be there," I say.

He leaves. I ignore my tears and keep working. I work through the night. I work through sunrise. Near noon, I float the coconuts out and lash them to the belly of the platform.

When I'm done with all ten, I look at my watch. Almost two o'clock.

I lash the supplies to the deck inside the lean-to. I unwrap the sail and test it against the breeze. I drop the center board, lift it, jump up and down on the lashed outriggers, kick at the rudder.

The raft is as finished as it's going to be.

I sit on my log in the circle and watch him read from the cookbook.

"He was an old man who fished alone in a skiff in the Gulf Stream and he had gone eighty-four days now without taking a fish."

I can't imagine how he does it. He must have known it by heart before Captain Andy's boat capsized. Maybe his insanity lets him dredge up the stories from the past. Still, it's one thing to memorize the eggs and ham story or remember a tale about a little girl and big red dog; it's something else entirely to remember word-for-word an entire novel.

Of course, I can't check it, but I'm sure he remembers it perfectly.

I sit and watch him turn the pages. His certainty, the smooth action of his fingertips, the way he slides his fingers up the side of the book and folds in the next page to wait for the next turning. It all says he knew the book completely, that if I ever made it home, I would find that particular edition on his shelves. When I looked at those pages, I would see that the last word he spoke before turning the page would be the last word on the page in the real book.

He peers through his glasses at the book. To him, it's real. Occasionally, he peers over his glasses at me and smiles. Even so, he never misses a word.

It's a long reading. I listen carefully while Santiago cuts bait and fishes. I take mental notes while he fights the great fish. I worry while he fights the sharks.

I sit as I did as a child, in awe at the spell of this man, my librarian.

When he finally puts his book down, he takes a long breath.

I take a long breath. "That was amazing," I say.

"Thank you, William," he says. Then he stands and looks through his glasses. "Do you think the library on the other side of Ganges Pond is still there?" he asks.

I'm stunned. I know he sees me as I am. I try to think of the right answer. His librarian's gaze makes me small, and I can't lie. "I don't know," I say.

"The tide is turning, William," he says. "You'll need to catch it if you want to get out of the bay tonight."

He's lucid. He's looking directly at me. He takes his glasses off and looks into my eyes. "You have everything you need to make it," he says.

For the first time since we crawled up onto the hot, white sand, my belly's cold. "We." I say. "We have everything we need to make it."

He puts his glasses back on and peers over the top.

"No," he says. "I am the librarian. I have my duties. The great Ganges Pond crossing is up to you, William. I could never leave my books."

Whatever lucidity he had for a moment is gone. I think again about knocking him out and carrying him to the raft. I'm stronger, taller.

He bends and gathers his invisible book from an invisible table.

It's my chance.

The perfection of his motion would make a great mime cry at his own incompetence. The impression of the size and shape of the volume is perfect. I feel the book almost as if I'm touching it myself.

He walks a few paces left, lifts a hand up to his eye-level, inserts the flat of his hand between two volumes in stacks I can't see, then nestles the *Old Man and the Sea* between them.

He turns back to me. He smiles. "The library is closing, William," he says. "I believe it is time for you to go."

I hesitate. I can't hurt him. I can't take him from his books.

"Thank you, Mr. Morton," I say. "I'll come back."

"I know you will, William," he says. "And William."

"Yes?"

"You will be nice to the new librarian, won't you?"

I nod and turn toward the sea.

Airport

by Janet Burroway

I keep stepping on the ugly map
of all our local comings and disappearings;
dingy—yellow, is it?—or I suppose
they call it "gold," with, surely, "garnet" flowers
or suns, whatever, and so do the tired arrivals
with their carry-ons, and the pickers-up
in their tanks and wrinkled shorts
and their carryings-on, the helium balloons
and welcome signs;
and us in our wrinkled shorts, already tired
to death of the, welcome, however, visitor—
he is not unwelcome, whoever he is, or she—
over the same carpet, from the same planes,
to the same luggage endlessly riding round
and round the creaking carousel.
And you,
arriving every time with him or her,

arriving every time
on your bouncing step
over the golden not-so-dingy-then,
and the luggage smelling leather-fresh,
and the carousel fresh-installed,
and your helium eyes
and your careless grin
into the wrinkled arms of my
welcome home.

Tests and Taxes

by Mike Jack Stoumbos

Hello! Welcome to your friendly neighborhood branch of the National Testing Center.

We've got just a few seconds before our allotted tour time begins, and I want to make sure that everyone is perfectly comfortable and settled on the conveyor platform. Don't worry--it moves at a very easy pace, and our automated guidance systems give plenty of warning for every major or minor transition, just like our electronic testing programs. There, you see that blinking green light? That means your tour is about to begin.

What's that? You're feeling nervous?

Oh, not about the tour; you mean an upcoming test. You don't need to feel bad about that. It's perfectly normal. Luckily, when you do come in for your official testing session, you will have the option of taking mood regulators to handle the anxiety.

No, we didn't supply any for the tour, but I'll be sure to pass your note to my supervisors.

It looks like almost everyone is settled in and ready to

go--

What's that ma'am?

No, you don't need to turn in your phone. In fact, you don't even have to power-off your personal devices--not anymore. You see, there once was a time when "any attempt to record or interfere with a testing environment" was a punishable offense, but, thankfully, we're well-past that. Not only does the new National Testing Center--or, your local NTC--operate publicly and transparently, but we also have low-level scrambling fields that disable all network connection to devices, except those pre-authorized for NTC use.

So feel free to <u>selfie</u> all you want! You can schedule anything you'd like to auto-post once your allotted tour time has expired.

Yes, we <u>want</u> people to know about the friendly, modern layout of our testing facilities. No more converted classrooms or stifling cubicles; no more secret warehouses. We want all of our test-takers to be in an ideal environment to ensure most accurate results. You know, the rooms in this complex were actually designed by psychologists to target pleasant emotions with color and shape.

In addition, here at the NTC, we far surpass standards for comfort, as you can see from our amazingly ergonomic testing chairs, which are visible on your left.

Keep in mind that if you happen to find something you like on our tour--which I'm sure you will--you can purchase it for yourself. All items, except for the tests themselves, are available for purchase though our eCatalog, which you can find on any of the public-access consoles. But, seriously, I highly recommend the testing chairs. I'm not ashamed to admit I now own six of them, one of which has been installed in my car as the new driver's seat. I'm thinking of getting a seventh for the bathroom.

How's that? You're wondering about the NTC supercomputer? Well, I can honestly say that I don't know if it will fit into your bathroom.

Yes, we like to kid here at the NTC, but if there is ever a hint of sarcasm in any of our test materials, we indicate with an orange highlight _and_ a footnote, just in case.

But, yes, the supercomputer. I suppose you _could_ buy one of your own, but you'd need a skyscraper to house its spire, a bunker for its records, and, well, an embarrassingly large stack of cash.

You'll be able to see the base of the supercomputer spire in just a few moments. Can I get a show of hands: how many of you are familiar with the NTC Supercomputer Test Administrator and Processor? Brilliant, well, how many of you knew that the NTC processes more data than the entirety of the International Space Program and the Transcontinental Securities Administration combined?

That's right, our supercomputer handles algorithms on a local, national, global, and solar-system level-- because how else would we be able to compare your results on each test item to those of billions of others. Meanwhile, the Space Program only has to manage a few extra-terran bases, and the occasional launch of one craft at a time. And the TSA? (Yes, I do mean the Transcontinental Securities Administration.) They get most of their information from NTC complexes like this one. How else would they know what kinds of potentially dangerous persons to look in on unless we provided them the test data?

I see that you're impressed. Or... perhaps that's concern. No need to worry about the TSA. If you were on a watch-list, you never would have been allowed into the facility in the first place.

And now we arrive at the base of the supercomputer's spire. Yes, young man, it is that "chimney-shaped thing" you saw on your drive here. In fact, it continues to extend out of the complex until it's more than two-thousand feet above ground level.

Doesn't it look majestic?

Why does it need to be that high? Naturally, for line of sight, and recently, so it can get past the interference of E-M-P and anti-nuclear-strike fields, in order to communicate with our NTC satellites directly.

Well, yes, I am aware that there are taller spires than our local site's--I do work for the NTC after all, and comparing quantitative data is what we do. But you wouldn't want to hear about how many people tested higher than you, now would you? And that is also something an NTC employee could provide for you.

How much did the supercomputers cost? Oh, you might have me on that one. It was a nationally-funded project that took literally billions of employee-hours to complete, and it was built on what was already state-of-the-art technology. It is difficult to put a price tag on. Which, I guess is one way of saying it's priceless.

Yes, I think it was a brilliant use of tax dollars.

Why invest so much in testing, you ask?

Well, with a global population approaching eleven figures and still climbing, it's really the only way to effectively track the progress and prowess of any individual, especially if you want to compare that individual--which we do.

What's that? Your grandma says that testing is a waste of time?

Well, of course it was back in her day. See, back then, it wasn't very well regulated, and everyone was using a different standard, and organizations were trying to <u>fake</u> their results by <u>lowering</u> their standards. So testing was not effective, and the costs that went into it had no positive outcomes--for anyone: students, teachers, governments.

But now, we've got it all figured out. Thanks to the Transcontinental Educational Constitution, we managed to re-standardize everything across the world, and even to our installations on Mars. We figured out the right factors, and we created the right tests to find them. By now, we know exactly how to track those who are most likely to innovate, to create, most likely to continue to learn and grow and advance science and industry.

And once we had the standards, we didn't stop there. We are constantly fine-tuning our testing methods, making minute adjustments every year--heck!--every day, so our tests are giving us, and you, the best information we can provide.

Because, really, what's the point of testing unless it gives you good data?

And you know what they say: "Good testing makes good data, and good data makes good teachers."

You hadn't heard that one? Well, now you have.

Speaking of which, if you look to your right, you will see some of our teacher-training facilities. Why, yes, there is a dormitory on-site for trainees enrolled in the intensive programs--it makes the process much more efficient.

Yes, all teachers have to be trained in the kinds of tests their students will be taking. Did you know that just a few decades ago, even that kind of obvious training was not required? And they wondered why their education system collapsed!

Now, thankfully, one-hundred-percent of teachers are properly prepared to teach to NTC standards--which are in line with Global Competitive Standards. And we make a point of selecting those teachers who will best be able to support the tests--excuse me, to support *the students* in taking the tests.

Of course the NTC handles teacher certification! You don't need to fret about that.

They have also learned all of the proper encouragement techniques, so that their children will be less frightened of national tests. Children, just like this young lady with her hand raised. Yes, what is your question?

What's that? What if you don't want to get tested?

Well... I guess, technically, you can choose not to attend a test session, just like you can choose not to eat. I don't think it'll do you much good.

There used to be this saying, that there were only two sure things in life: death and taxes. And, well, the <u>death</u> part is no longer a "sure thing". These days, if you have the means to finance it, you can extend your life indefinitely. There is no age-limit to the rejuvenation treatments as far as we know--and here at the NTC, we know quite a bit.

No, really, one of our CEOs celebrated her one-hundred-fifty-fifth birthday just last month. She still has to pay taxes, and she still comes in for regular testing to make sure she stays above par.

For example, to your left, you will see one of our facilities for comprehensive physical-wellness testing. Sure, you don't <u>have</u> to come in for that, but if you ever want to try out for a sport, get a pregnancy permit, or take a trip to Mars, there's no alternative.

Well, sure, it's fair! Listen, if the government is going to invest valuable funds and population space for <u>your</u> desires, the least you can do is spend an afternoon in a testing center. Not to mention that every time you come in for a test, you get a free voucher for a VR session or a film screening. Come on! Who says the NTC doesn't give with both hands?

Well, I definitely wouldn't say that the NTC <u>punishes</u>

people for failing to take requisite tests, but if you are interested in more information on that subject, we can refer you to our onsite legal offices.

The reality is, most schools and work environments, as well as insurance providers, require consistent testing. Citizens over eighteen years of age <u>do</u> have the right to choose to not receive higher education, or to not be employed, or to not be insured. Considering that the only cost is coming in for a few test sessions, it seems silly that anyone would--

But I'm getting off topic! Who wants to see the complimentary cafeteria? Oh, sorry, not for those on the tour, just our test-takers. We want to make sure they're all well-fed.

What's that, sir?

Oh, you still want to talk about <u>that</u>? Alright.

You know, there's a bit of confusion on some of the NTC's practices and what kinds of things we can do here. As an employee of the NTC, I am quite aware that some people are--shall we say--resistant toward our required regular testing policies. These individuals also have a tendency to exaggerate about what the government does with the NTC test data.

For one thing, I can assure you that there is no "too smart"--it's not like that twentieth-century short-story about the boy getting executed for exceeding the national intelligence standards. Oh, you weren't familiar with that one?

The point is that testing is never like any of the

naysayers and their horror stories would have you believe. I know they can be amusing fantasies, but truthfully you're never going to be pressed into a career path because of an NTC test.

For example, you could discover that you have genius-level math acumen, which would make so many colleges and career-paths possible. But you could still decide that you would rather be--I don't know--a baker. The national tests are all about opening doors, not closing them.

Could you repeat that? I didn't catch it.

Oh, well, I guess I did hear you right, but I suppose that's another misconception we need to address.

No, the NTC does not authorize the "extermination of the useless." What a horrid thing to say.

What? No, it is obviously not "the same". <u>No longer paying for</u> someone's food, housing, or healthcare is not the same thing as killing them.

When the Transcontinental Educational Constitution was established, the writers saw the need for universal-basic-income and care. They agreed that some of the necessities, as well as healthcare and education, would be provided to all citizens by governments. But to a point.

Of course, those services can't be provided indefinitely. There is a maximum age for receiving free government aid--and I'm happy to tell you, that our country boasts the third highest free-care age in the world.

Beyond that, people are expected to pay for

themselves if they want to keep reaching for those ninety-ninth-percentile years.

Ah, yes, you heard right: the cutoff age is considerably lower for those who refuse NTC testing.

Oh, there's really no reason to complain about it. After all, if you fail to pay taxes, you might get fined or go to prison. And if you fail to show up to a test, you don't qualify for many of the amenities our government is otherwise happy to provide for you.

And if you <u>fail</u> the test? Well, here at the NTC, we don't deal in <u>failing</u> test scores. We show your percentile, areas of expertise, and areas for improvement.

And I suppose if your company or school requires a certain score from an NTC exam, then you could say that you fail if you don't meet that score. <u>You</u> could say it; I couldn't.

And government benefits? Ah, you can find out about the requisite scores for your individual city or county, but those are not set by the NTC.

I'm sorry, I'm hearing a lot of defeatist comments, and I feel a need to chime in: "What's the point of trying?" Well, you're acting as if your test is a foregone conclusion. That is a very negative attitude, and we have counselors who are equipped to handle that.

It's always best to try your best. After all, you fail one-hundred percent of the tests you don't take.

No, I'm not sure if that's the original quote or a paraphrase, but I can look it up in our extensive database.

Hmm? You're not convinced? Well, you certainly

have a right to voice your objections, but I'm afraid there's little I can do with them. Comments and feedback for the NTC are officially handled by experts, and they can be reached through a designated feedback terminal.

Why, yes, you do have to exit the tour in order to use a designated feedback terminal at this time.

What's that, sir?

No, sir, I don't think of myself as a fascist, but if you'd like to leave a comment or suggestion--

Sir, I'm going to have to ask you to please refrain from further comments, so that others can enjoy the-- Well, now, that is uncalled for.

Sir, the NTC certainly does not deal in death! None of our policies involve killing people.

Sir, I'm afraid that your derisive remarks will need to be handled by other members of the NTC staff. And here they come.

Ladies and gentlemen, approaching from our right, you will see a fine example of NTC security guards arriving to escort this gentleman from the tour. The NTC employs the finest security forces, primarily for parents who are worried about their children's test results, and, as of such, they are trained in a variety of soothing tactics. As you can see, our guard has just peacefully coaxed that unruly gentleman to sleep with a little bit of pressure to the correct nerve cluster. Thank you very much.

I'm extremely sorry you had to witness that. You'll be glad to know the gentleman in question will wake up, feeling refreshed, in our patented aroma-therapeutic recovery room. He will also receive a refund for the tour.

I'm not going to lie: even I have faked a few headaches in order to take a good nap in the recovery room. So if anyone else feels like checking out a spa-grade relaxation space, now would be a great time to make an unpleasant scene.

No? Alright then, let's move on to--

Oh, you still want to talk about <u>that</u>?

Look, I'll try to address this one more time, but then we should get back to the tour agenda. (We've already missed three major tour points, and typically, the NTC advises against skipping content.)

<u>So</u>: You say you want to live forever, but you want to avoid taking the tests.

Well, let me ask you something: how do you expect to get the money to finance such a long life? In order to begin the best career paths, you need a great college education, but you can't get into any colleges without the NTC's academic tests.

If you want to be a celebrity--first of all, good luck--but I can tell you that no producer or agent will take you if they can't see some NTC records.

Why? Well, if nothing else, to make sure you're not going to keel over from a heart attack. But more than that, the personality profiles and the mental aptitude tests can give them a great idea of your range as an actor or singer or any other kind of entertainer.

Did I mention that the NTC does arts certification testing? You can scroll through the touchscreen to see the different courses. Why, I know about arts programs firsthand from my Announcer/Commentator cert--couldn't you tell?

And, when it comes to extending your life--and I don't just mean staying healthy through your seventies or eighties; I mean returning to the physical prime of life--clearly, you need the NTC. To even qualify for a rejuvenation treatment <u>conference</u>, you have to have recently taken both mental and physical aptitude tests. I don't know of any rejuvenation clinics that accept non-NTC records; and I certainly wouldn't trust any so-called clinics that did.

<u>And</u>, if you want your company or even the government to pay for your rejuvenation, you have to show them that you'll continue to be more of an asset than a burden, and how can you hope to have a good career-projection model without an NTC career-projection test?

By <u>asset</u>, yes, I mean performing a task that couldn't easily be absorbed by a robot.

Well, I'm flattered to hear you say that. I have been working on precision elocution, but, no, I am not a robot. The range of customer reactions is--as of yet--too broad for a robot to properly handle.

Okay... I guess if there <u>were</u> robots running the tours, then the National Testing Centers would probably program ones who could seem effectively human, so that transitions sound natural to the average customer, which would be something that we could test after all. We couldn't really call ourselves a *Testing Center* if we couldn't manage a Turing test, now could we?

If you would like to know just how many different assessments we offer, I invite you to schedule a free client-intake meeting in our registration building, which is just ahead.

Yes, Registration <u>is</u> the first thing you can see coming into the complex, which means we have nearly finished the circuit.

You didn't notice we had already turned around? Well, here at the NTC, we strive to make all of our transitions as smooth as possible so that you don't feel bombarded by new or unexpected material.

In the corner of the console screens, you will find a series of options for the conclusion of our tour. You may also download a complete transcript of the tour, many terms of which have been highlighted and linked to further information. I also highly recommend clicking on our eCatalog and Registration pages before you go.

As we arrive at the station, this is your final opportunity to ask questions and to double-check any questions that you have already asked.

Why is there a written record of everything that has been said on the tour? Well, the NTC is always looking for ways to improve our customer-interaction, and the Transcontinental Securities Administration (or TSA) likes to review these records for signs of any risk or security breach.

Would it make you feel safer to know that there are also visual and audio recordings of this tour? It certainly makes me feel safer. After all, the NTC test sites and supercomputers have to have the best security measures available--and we do, you know. Have the best security systems--okay, excluding a few megalomaniac celebrities and rulers who think that their lives are more important than information about billions of people. But we tend to ignore those. Here at the NTC, we also know that good data often consists of eliminating outliers.

Conspiracy Theorists

by Koraly Dimitriadis

I get depressed listening to conspiracy theorists babble
I try to hold the space for them as best I can
What is it they actually want me to do with this
    information?
I'm neither here nor there, man
Are your theories rooted in any kind of fact?
Like who are your sources?
And who are *their* sources?

Lonely nights are long, Facebook pings yet another un-
    invited message.
Scroll my news feed, stumble over rambles of friends I
    once respected,
I refrain, yet my journalistic, investigative brain can't
    resist the deep dive deciphering
A click leads to a click leads to a click leads to...where am
    I?
What does *this* have to do with anything?
Stop trying to yank me down the rabbit hole you seem to

have disappeared into
What is it you actually want me to do with all this
    information?
I'm just trying to put all my energy into stopping the days
    from spinning
Okay, so some of it may be true,
like I believe you, sort of, I'm not sure,
probably, I don't know,
but you're speaking at me
like you want me to do something with all this,
something of importance,
like start a crusade to take over
the one world government
you claim is trying to do all this
Maybe they are, I don't know
But what do you want me to do about it?
I'm just trying to put one foot in front of the other
5G, Bill Gates, New World Order, vaccines
Yeah, if one comes I probably will get jabbed
What else do you expect me to do?
There's a pandemic and I can't leave my house
Seriously, my brain hurts, help!
Give me a break, conspiracy theorist
My head hurts. Bad. Like the room is spinning.
I'm off to bed, to sleep off your words

The 100th Heroine

by Heather S. Ransom

Running away from him, she screams, clutching her necklace. Glancing back, she can just see him, the knife glistening at his side as he breathes heavily. She reaches the door, fumbles with the lock. She can't seem to make it work. He laughs.

It is a horrible, demeaning, misogynistic laugh. She is so tired of that laugh. If she wasn't so fucking scared, she would roll her eyes. Grasping at the door handle, she shakes it as hard as she can. She keeps hearing her mother's voice in her head, "Make it realistic, Diana. You have to sell it to the crowd." Hearing Vincent's thudding footsteps, she screams again.

Spinning, she flattens her back against the rough door. Glancing up, she can see her mother leaning forward from her seat, gripping the railing in the dimly lit balcony, that asinine grin on her face. The same one she wore on the day the letter arrived.

"It's every girl's dream, Diana." Her mother had been looking in a mirror, applying lipstick. "In my eighteenth year, my own mother so wanted me to have the role. But, Sophia Larus was chosen. Her mother went on to be president of the Ladies Auxiliary for the next six years. Six years. Can you believe that? And, now you, you have been chosen. There's no higher honor you can bring to our family." Her mother dabbed at an edge that threatened to bleed beyond the well-manicured line.

Diana had felt sick to her stomach. She sat down at the table. Honor? That was not it felt like to her. It felt like... like... death.

"Diana? Diana? What on earth is wrong with you?" Her mother looked at her expectantly.

"I... I... I don't think I can do this."

"What? Of course, you can. You're our family's last chance. It was such a disappointment when your sisters weren't selected. Poor Aurelia, she was depressed for weeks. And then, we thought Antoinette would be a shoo-in. That Mills girl wasn't very realistic. Antoinette would have been so much better."

Her mother's voice fades from Diana's mind. This is the part when she really needs to focus. Vincent's eyes dance as he slides towards her. The orchestra in the pit somewhere below plays ominous music. It is heavy, almost suffocating. He fondles the knife, sneering. He is so excited for what is to come.

"I've decided I'm not doing it, Mother. I can't. I won't. There are too many other things I want to do—"

"That's enough, Diana. Think of your family. Think of what it will do for us. You can't be that selfish. Think of—"

"But, Mother, please! Listen to me! I—"

"Diana, we all have sacrifices we make. For family. For tradition. For community. You know that. The annual retelling of this story is our most important event."

"But Mother, anything else, please, listen to me! I—"

"This is the way it's been done for years. For longer than any of us can remember. My grandmother told me stories about it that her grandmother had shared with her. It's our way to pay tribute to the girl who saved our town. Everything she and her family gave. And, more importantly, it ensures that each of us remember how crucial it has always been to do our part in upholding the sanctity of protecting our community."

"But just because it's always been done doesn't mean—"

"Enough, Diana! Go practice your lines." The look in her eyes had told Diana the conversation was over. Annoyance. Expectation. Anger.

 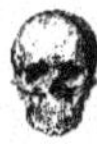 

A startling crash causes her to jump. What? This is not in the script. Diana notices Vincent is not on his mark. Shit. He is improvising again. He thinks it makes him such a great actor. Diana moves back to center stage. Her eyes scan the dark edges that creep toward her. She hears rustling. He is there, just beyond where she can see. Her skin crawls. Her breath quickens. Her heart pounds.

"I've never actually personally known someone who's got the part. I mean the Heroine. Your mom's application must have been super awesome. I don't think my mom put more than ten minutes into mine. God, she's always so busy with her own stuff." Jolie continued to file her nails as she ambled on. "Remember a few years ago when Gerald Baldwin had that small role? He's the only one from our school that I can think of. Unless you go way back."

Diana was not really listening to her. Before all of this, they were not close. Not even someone she would have considered a friend. But once the names of the cast were announced, Jolie dropped by her house almost every day. Everyone wanted to hang out with Diana since she had been "chosen." Like she had had a choice.

"I was thinking about turning the role down, you know, focus on other things I could do in the future—"

Jolie laughed. A snarky, irritating sound. "You can't be serious! You'll be memorialized. Your picture will hang in the town center. You're going to be the 100th Heroine. You know what a big deal they're making out of this year with it being the centennial celebration and all. I mean, we all know each year is important, but you scoring the role this year...," her voice trailed off momentarily as she locked eyes with Diana. "You'll be famous. And that's forever."

Diana dropped her eyes. Jolie paused. Diana's voice was soft, only a whisper, when she said, "I could give the role to you...."

Jolie's face feigned surprise. "What? That would never happen. Once the choice has been made, it's never been reversed."

"But—"

"Come on, Di. Live it up. Take advantage of the fame. Everyone knows your name right now. You can get anything you want."

But Jolie had been wrong. What Diana wanted was not an option because everyone expected the show to go on.

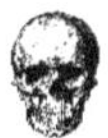

Diana feels Vincent's breath on the back of her neck before she hears him. Damn, he can be so quiet for such a big guy. Then that shitty laugh again. Back on cue. She spins and jumps away. She knows she is supposed to fall down in front of him, but her legs refuse to follow the script. Surprise flashes across Vincent's face, then a quick smile. Like he approves. Like she is the one improvising now. Maybe she is.

"Come on, Diana. Let's run through your lines again."

Her mother's frown had permeated her entire face. "Can't you try a bit harder? You need to be excellent."

"Mother, I told you I'm not cut out for this. I'm not brave. I'm not an actress. I'm not—"

"You are what you choose to be, Diana. You can make this role yours. Throw yourself into character." Her mother's arms had flailed as she droned on about the significance of the role of the Heroine. "You really must try to channel the Heroine, honey. Think of how clever she was keeping that maniac fixated on her until the constable could get there to arrest him. She saved the town. The killings had gone on for months. Just imagine what might have happened if she hadn't been brave enough. If she had thought she wasn't... good enough." She droned on.

"It's the same play every year. The only thing that ever changes are the names of the actors. Everyone already knows the entire plot," Diana mumbled to herself.

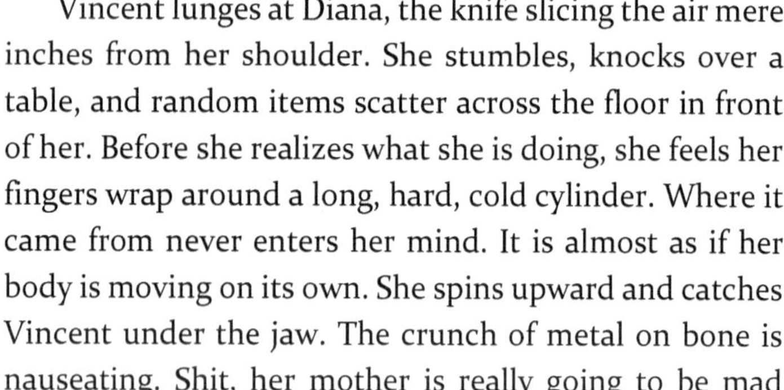

Vincent lunges at Diana, the knife slicing the air mere inches from her shoulder. She stumbles, knocks over a table, and random items scatter across the floor in front of her. Before she realizes what she is doing, she feels her fingers wrap around a long, hard, cold cylinder. Where it came from never enters her mind. It is almost as if her body is moving on its own. She spins upward and catches Vincent under the jaw. The crunch of metal on bone is nauseating. Shit, her mother is really going to be mad now.

"This is it, Diana. Tonight's the night. Everything we've worked for. It all comes down to this. Are you ready? You're ready. We've practiced. You'll be sensational. I know you will. I wonder how long it will take them to come talk to me about being President of the Ladies Auxiliary. Maybe even as soon as tomorrow. You think?" Her mother's eyes had danced wild with excitement. She was not really talking to Diana. Just at her. As usual.

Diana stood, tugging at the long black skirt as it caught on one of the legs of her dressing room table. She pulled it free, noticing a small snag with frayed threads exposed. Not that it really mattered.

"Goodbye, Mother."

"Oh. Yes. Of course. It's about that time, isn't it? I should be heading to my seat. I don't want to miss a minute of this." Her mother smiled at her. "You do look excruciatingly beautiful, Diana."

"Thank you, Mother."

"I'm so proud of you."

Unfucking believable.

From the corner of her eye, Diana sees her mother throw her hands up in front of her face. She is standing now. Then a roar from Vincent nearly stops her heart. They are so off-script.

A thought registers in her mind. Screw the script. Deny them the expected performance. Improvise. Make this her show.

Most of the audience is on their feet now. Guttural yelling. Fists in the air. Diana swings the metal bar as hard as she can toward Vincent several more times, grunting aloud from the exertion. Vincent takes an awkward step back. Then two more.

She can do this. She can change this. No more girls have to—

This time Vincent side steps. His hand, seemingly from nowhere, appears in front of her. A simple, nimble little move that Diana doesn't see coming. A fierce, wet heat blossoms in her chest. Not really pain, which is strange. She had been scared it would hurt.

Stepping back, Vincent howls in victory. In one last defiant moment, she leans into him. Her lips moving close to his smug face. His lips move toward her.

She coughs hard.

Red droplets cover his face and begin to trickle down. For a moment, he is frozen, in that time. In that place. Then he laughs that laugh, and her defiance drains. She staggers away from him. Back to the script.

Diana slumps to the ground. Slides to a prone position, like they practiced, but this time a metallic taste fills her mouth. She grasps at her necklace, giving it a jerky tug. It is slippery now. But the chain gives, spraying beads chaotically across the floor, small red trails following until they roll lifelessly to a stop. For the one hundredth time in one hundred years. Nothing has changed.

At that moment, Jackson Marks bursts onto the stage in his crisply pressed constable's uniform, roughly wrestling Vincent to the ground and into handcuffs. The lights dim and then come back up. Deafening applause erupts. They had got what they wanted.

With effort, Diana tilts her head slightly toward the balcony. Her mother, beaming and waving to those below her, makes her way toward the stairs to come to the stage where she will take the final bow for Diana. Her friends around her are smiling and touching her as she passes. Apparently, Diana's off-script antics have not done too much damage. Maybe her mother will be president of the Ladies Auxiliary tomorrow after all.

Diana lets her eyes drift to her hand now resting in a widening pool of blood on the floor next to her chest. A deep hatred fills her as a blackness seeps in at the edges of her vision. She was just one more dead girl. And there would be another next year. And the year after that.

They called her the Heroine. Right. She could not even save herself. Just another silly girl, too scared, too dumb, too naïve to say no.... and, for the first time, she realized that was probably why they had chosen her. She had never been good at saying no.

Had she really thought she could change it? That she had that kind of power? Who was she kidding? No one changed the show. The audience had never needed her, the 100th Heroine, to save anyone. She didn't need to sell anything now. They just needed her to die.

Stupid Moveable Organs

by Kate Maxwell

My tongue creeps around the edges
of a crater; freshly gouged and shocking
in my gum. This open wound needs time
and isolation to heal but, oh, such shark
bait to a moveable organ tingling at the seep
of blood. Twitching to poke and plunder
all for a quick lick, a soft sensation.
But I've no pity for its simple urges
and what it wants, is every impulse eased.

The dentist clearly states the damaging
desires of my tongue and warns,
Do not disturb the clot, be careful not
to bite your lip. Expect a little oozing.
But how to make the fleshy fool
inside my mouth, be still? Keep distance
know the risks of infection spread
and understand its duty to the mouth?
My tongue rebuffs the notion of contagion

knows nothing of science, denies that it's
attached by skin, by loyalty and tendons
and claims liberty to choose its own path.
Yet, while I bleed, it bleeds too.
It probes until it's numb and tasteless.

And now all festers: toothless, weak.
Just so many weeping holes
once rooted in white bright beliefs.
Warnings that may have saved,
our stupid moveable organs, ignored.

Oracles

by Janet Burroway

He will ask her tonight. She *knows* this. The sky is full of auguries—a full-blown blossom on the spindly magnolia at the corner of Grove and Bleeker, a shooting star last night over Washington Square—even the date, May 8, 1958, is an elegant symmetry, and in the European form would be a palindrome: 8-5-58. Also the anniversary of V-E day, as he has pointed out. (The *thirteenth* anniversary, true; you can carry these games too far.) He will ask her and then there will be no more tension between them, none of those dark moments when she doesn't know what she has done wrong, but something. He will disguise his proposal with an ironic look and a negative construction: *Not that this is particularly sudden*, or *I don't suppose you'd have any interest in*...and then it will be there, and done, and the future laid out before them.

He will meet her in front of Zabar's and they'll have supper with Mrs. Puig, even though that will rush them. (Why should they go to his mother's before a show if it's not a statement of intent?) The show is called *Nickels in*

May, which must be a musical though she hasn't heard of it. She can see the stage, bare boards full of young people in primary colors and bobby socks, a full-blooded, full-throated American belting out. Yes, and a young Negro chorine with a great bubble of black hair, like Kuli Moyala from his lab at Columbia, who wears bangles above the elbow and batik robes of sass-reds and blood-browns. All the Negroes Simone has met till now have their hair ironed into waves or page-boys, but Kuli wears a narrow band of beaded stuff around a sprouting of charred oak, so defiantly beautiful that Simone feels like a Miss Milquetoast in her presence.

She has actually eaten milk toast. She didn't believe it existed, but Mrs. Puig—she must learn to call her Hester now, or even *Mom?*— served it on a Sunday night, a bowl of warm milk with a slice of buttered white toast drowning in it. An amazing thing. Simone had thought her years in England showed her all there was for mush and bland.

That she hasn't heard of the musical is not surprising. Martin knows about off-Broadway things, quirky Village things, loft-shoestring productions. He knows the starving avant-garde. She nips back through Washington Square, sweating a little because she needs all six of these books this weekend, and they're heavy. The Kitto alone—*Form and Meaning in Drama*—weighs two pounds in its library binding. Her brain, too, is a little top-heavy with all those bird-portents and the ravings of Cassandra. She turns into Eighth Street, past Julia's Gems, not pausing and not turning her head because if the ring is still there (the slender circle with the single bend, like a golden scribble; the single black pearl at its zenith), she doesn't want to know. And if it isn't there, what, all the same, would it prove for certain?

She hadn't intended to marry. She had spent so much time in other people's squabbling families, and then the sultry closeness of a women's quarters, that she had thought herself only interested in freedom, only in her own intricate train of thought. Now, here, in America, the fact of loneliness has not surprised her but the force of it has. The lack of purpose in a thought unshared, the pull of laziness when she lives in reference only to herself— all that was unexpected. Meanwhile everyone she knows is pairing off. Everyone is lifted on a tide toward marrying, having children. The tide is inexorable. At some point every other possible way of being is swept along.

Nor had she intended to be a teacher. She had wanted to be an actor, or at least to immerse herself in the kind of life she believed actors had. Well, the classroom is a kind of stage. And after all, isn't it the stories that always held her? Martin teases her, pretending to be a determinist: *blood will out*. But wasn't it a story that had led her father to be a professor of English literature, even if, in Liege, the subject had to be dressed up with a proficiency in Middle High German and Old Norse? Whereas here she could study Norman Mailer if she chose. She has chosen Euripides.

She hurries down the half-flight to the Grove Street

basement and lets herself in. She kicks off her loafers and pedal pushers and stands in her panties pouring a handful of seed in the cage—shaped like a wicker wedding cake—where a Javanese Temple bird called Ginsberg scolds from side to side. The advantage of this one room, a half-story underground, is that if you adjust the blinds at an angle nobody can see in. The disadvantage, apart from ninety dollars a month, is that car exhaust and passing feet and the slightest breeze sift in the airborne detritus of New York. The guy she sublet from said, "It's a fact you get more air below street level than higher up." How can you buy such a line? Nevertheless she still believes it, and that the air in question contains body ash, glass, concrete, carbon dioxide, sweat-impregnated lint and pulverized dog doo. Simone sweeps twice a day. Everything she owns is overlaid with a layer of wasteland.

Not her clothes. She has tacked a sheet over the skimpy burlap curtain at the closet. She takes the sheet down when she entertains. Now she slings it over her shoulder to dig into the shallow cavity and spread out the Merry Widow bra, a pair of pale beige stockings, the new drop-waisted linen on which she spent the weekend and over twelve dollars if you count the zipper.

She showers in the grubby cubicle, leans into the Merry Widow (another extravagance, but also a necessity, like armor), and reaches back to hook all thirty five miniature fish hooks from wingblade to base of spine. This is a heady time she knows to be heady at the time—

the first time in her life she has had cleavage, for instance, thanks to the Merry Widow. Putting it on lets you know what it feels like to have your hands tied behind you while being hoisted onto a beam. But when the hooks are done, when she bends and shakes, settles her breasts into the underwires and straightens up, she has a handspan of waist and lifted globes between which you could pinch a finger. It's hard to breathe.

The dress is pale bone Irish Moygashel, the real thing, bought from Art-Max discount fabrics on Thirty-Eighth. She has cut the top princess line and the skirt in six gores flaring from just the height of her hip joints, all the seams top-stitched in gunmetal grey. She has also laid out for mid-heel linen pumps, which will probably not survive six blocks of New York streets, but she can't wear her stilettos with Martin; he's too short. She back-combs her hair (not much; it's so thick it takes on volume at once) and brushes the top layer smooth.

When she looks at herself, it'll do. It's good. Hair bouffant, eyes clear, stance solid on her own two feet. He likes forceful women; he praises her for poise. She looks to make sure she has a dime for the subway, slings a cardigan over her arm and drives home the key.

She is excited but not nervous, going to meet Martin. After a two-year-long shuffle of lame dates, aggressive jocks, conversations so stilted that she found herself squandering her own history just to have something to talk about, Martin put her at her ease. He likes to talk ideas, not anecdotes. He knows the difference between wit and jokes. He wants to pick her brain about literature, to find the connective tissue between his subject and hers. They had exhausted most of B.F. Skinner and The New Criticism before he ever held her hand. And then he can be, deliciously, at one and the same time both romantic and wry. He has a temper, yes, that sometimes flares out of nothing and makes her both anxious and— admit it—embarrassed for him.

In just this hour the air has changed color. *Twi-light*, a word she loves, from the Old English *two-light*; *double light*. It is day and night at once; the opposites meet, and New York energy rises in the clash of them. Stone takes on a steel sheen, mica in the concrete gives off sparks. Everyone is charging away from work or off to play. She not least, clattering down the subway stairs, breathing shallow against the metal stays.

She loves the city, the urgency, the challenge. But she does not see herself and Martin living in the city. On the contrary, New Hampshire or Vermont, a small college town and a small cottage-y sort of house, a garden although to tell the truth neither of them is a gardener. She sees them in the kitchen rather, he with a dish towel in hand, holding forth on his latest experiments in Skinnerism while toddlers and a dog dawdle on the floor in the twilight. This makes her laugh.

She spots him a block away, sucking on a cigarette under the Z in *Zabar's*. Martin Carlo Puig runs everywhere, his compact body a fist of energy. But when—as often happens because he concentrates as hard as he runs—she spots him first, what comes off him is a melancholy of that same intensity. Unaware he is being watched, Martin sinks into himself, to some place that draws her like a labyrinth. Some people find Martin remote—Kuli Moyala calls him *iceman*—but Simone understands his secret grief, and when the dark mood takes him she wants to thread into his sorrow, track to the core of it, find the string to pull him out.

When Martin was seventeen, his father—having first made sure that Martin would arrive at his apartment at a given hour—had steadied a pistol at his palate and blown off the back of his head, precisely in the white-carpeted vestibule. For Martin, this memory, the cruelty of it, is an obsession; and for Simone, absorbing it has become a way of life. Martin accepts that she has scarcely any memory of her father, that formal man, and is as content to focus on Martin's loss as he is to let her.

Now, though, Martin merely grinds the butt under his heel. "Jesus. Gorgeous," he very satisfactorily says. "It's not Sardi's, you know." But he himself, a dapper dresser, is in a blazer and a slice of oxblood tie. He has muscular dark hair, broad brow, thick neck and shoulders, a fighter's body though he's a philosopher-scholar in psychology. His praise warms her. Nobody has ever before loved her being smart. All the women at Cambridge were smart. Martin likes her British-inflected whimsy and her tenacious habit of mind. *And* he likes her Merry Widow waistline. *Gorgeous.*

Martin's ancestry suggests a journey northward, from a Spanish great-great-grandfather who married a Basque, all the way up Europe, across the Atlantic to New England

and to Martin, who is set to carry on this tradition via Simone in the direction of ethnic pallor. The Mediterranean strain survives in him: the name, the darkness, the fierce pride. He might as well be Greek, Simone thinks. *Hellenic.* His power thrills her, a man with authority enough to want a strong woman. A runner's thighs, and that interior dark space no one can invade.

"*M'sieur le Puig,*" she says and pecks him at the temple. He smells of citrus and nicotine. "How come we're meeting here?"

"I thought we'd get some decent coffee and a stinky cheese. I can't stand that stuff she lays out. Maybe we could take some garlic and toss it in the soup."

"It would hurt her feelings."

"Her feelings? How would anybody know?"

His contempt for his mother causes her a flicker of unease, although she shares it, or because she shares it. She forms her face into a conspiratorial smile. They pick a loaf of rye, a brie, a bottle of Bordeaux. They will shop this way in the country, Simone foresees, always together, making a celebration of sustenance, making an aesthetic out of need.

Mrs. Puig has the glamorous address of 100 Riverside Drive, though her apartment is on the wrong, no-river-view, side, so they cross Eighty-fifth for a minute to look at the Hudson in twilight, the shining sludge of it and the bone-bright rise of the Palisades across. He lights another cigarette and gives her one. There's a little chill, and she wills him to put his arm around her, but Martin is not susceptible to telepathy. In the bald mud at their feet, a brown bird is pulling on a worm. Like a worm in a cartoon, the fat elastic stretches and snaps back, and the bird pulls again until the worm slips free. She raises her eyes beyond the bird to the slow water, and she says, without any premonition that she will say this, "We lived on the river in Liege."

She remembers a balustrade of concrete or stone, the band of slow water narrower than the Hudson, the line of buildings—houses?—on the bank beyond.

Martin replies, "We'll travel as soon as we have money. We'll go all over Europe. We'll go back there."

She says nothing. On the ground in front of them the bird has won this time; another time the worm, another time the mud. It's all the stuff of bird-signs, grist for an oracle. She cartwheels her cardigan over her shoulders and recites in the direction of the river: "*The sea is there, and who shall drain its yield? It breeds / precious as silver, ever of itself renewed, / The purple ooze wherein our garments shall be dipped.*'"

Martin laughs. "You're not planning a swim, I hope?"

"It's Clytaemnestra. She just means that purple dye comes from sea plants—anemones or something. But of course she's also planning to stab him in his robes."

"Ah, subtext," Martin says with a mock leer. Martin approves of her doing the Greeks because those old dramas concerned themselves with action. He thinks the moderns intrude on psychology, which is his domain.

"*Lord of the ways, my ruin!*'" she cries. "*You have undone me once again, and utterly,*'" and they turn back up the street and wave to the doorman and step into the bronze Deco cage of the elevator.

Mrs. Puig opens the door at once. "Martin-Simone?" She peers and beckons. She is a tiny woman, fragile-seeming but aggressively so, like an antique windup toy, all grind and clatter. She's old; sixty-five, Simone thinks. A smell of poached fish wafts from behind her—"Come, come"—and she manages to convey that they are wasting heat by standing in the hall, although God knows it's too hot inside. She closes the door and offers each of them a paper cheek.

Vast, by New York standards, apartment 11E opens off both sides of one long hall ending in a generous suite with a dressing alcove. It's a solid turn-of-the-century building, but this particular apartment is furnished in a severe style it would be impossible to understand if you didn't know that Martin's father was a *Bauhaus* architect. He was, at one time, one of the few Americans acknowledged in the European circle, though his reputation declined somewhat between the time he left Martin and his mother in '38 and his suicide in '49.

His widow now houses here a collection of memorial chrome and canvas. The table is a concrete slab on pillars. The rugs are hard and plain. The only comfortable chair in the living room is a bent-pipe *chaise* you can't get up out of in a Merry Widow bra. *Form follows function* Simone admires in a theoretical way, but it strikes her as a dubious goal unless a chair serves the function of *comfortable to sit on.*

The friendliest piece of furniture is the blond wood cabinet housing the TV set that Mr. Puig did not live to see. Crowded on top of it—as if Mrs. Puig dares to clutter only this one alien space—are a hodge-podge of family photographs in dime store frames, several of Martin as a boy, in sailor suit, cowboy hat, graduation gown. Simone tries to recall such a picture of herself. Perhaps with her mother or her father, perhaps on the mantelpiece in Liege? Was there a mantelpiece in Liege?

The only thing in the apartment intended for décor is a *photomontage* called "Indische Tänzerin," *Indian Dancer*, though there is no dancer in it, and nothing Indian. It's of a woman's head in teal, and silver-gray, with images severed and recombined: a French film actress as Joan of Arc, a fragment of an African mask, a sand dune, knives and spoons. The actress's single eye is closed in sleep or grief or ecstasy. The mask's eye is open in the blind openness of stone. The parts don't fit together in any way that makes sense, and yet this cobbled-together thing is breathtakingly itself. Its brokenness makes it whole.

"I love this piece," Simone always says, because she does, and because Mrs. Puig always brightens.

"Hannah Höch was the only woman that the Dadaists were willing to accept among them!"

Simone touches the lower right corner with the initials "H.H." and the year of her own birth. "I love it," she says again.

"Of course, my husband never cared for the Dadaists. They were too irrational for him. He thought they were frivolous. And I didn't often go against his tastes. He was the artist." Her eyes are suddenly metallic, and Simone sees some complicated feeling behind their shine: mischief?—possibly shot through with rage?

"He thought people should be consistent. He liked *mesura*—that's Italian for measured, proportional. He said it often, *mesura* this and *mesura* that."

She's confiding in me, Simone recognizes. Martin calls it a *momologue.*

"I bought it myself! Well, I saved up a little bit here and there, and then I had my father's small inheritance, which wasn't enough, but that money *was* rightly mine!" She turns, momentarily exultant, to the kitchen, and Simone follows her, bemused. The Dadaists? It's hardly what she'd expect from her future mother-in-law. Perhaps she'll have time to think about it later.

"It's nearly ready," says Mrs. Puig, hovering at the kitchen counter. "I know you have to go, but these potatoes will *not* get done." Anxious and anxiety-producing as a way of life, she wrings her hands over the perfidy of the potatoes, and Simone laughs, feeling herself expand with good will and competence.

"Let me speak to them," she says. "They probably don't understand the assignment."

"Don't sweat it," Martin says. We don't have to be there till nine. I'm going to go check what mail has come for me."

That's odd. What sort of show doesn't start till nine?

The kitchen is done in some shiny white stuff, a clinic

for the evisceration of pits and bones. Simone dons an apron, and the two of them fall easily into poking, draining, decanting together, even though Mrs. Puig follows Simone's least movement with a wipe-up cloth.

"How have you been...Mrs. Puig?"

"I can't complain." This belied by a flinch, a tucked chin. *Subtext.* "I'm not altogether sure I'm eating right."

"You should have a big Porterhouse and a double ice cream sundae."

Mrs. Puig does not *get* teasing. 'No, no, no. It wouldn't suit me. I'm not like you youngsters. Martin and his cast-iron constitution...!" She dishes up the fish— skate, by the look of it, snowy meat on a fan of cartilage. And she launches into speech, a whirring of the mechanism behind the wind-up voice. "People have to work at it to find out what suits them. For years, I followed Gaylord Hauser's regime, but my husband, now, it didn't suit him at all. He wasted on it. He lost muscle."

"It's a long time ago," Simone says gently. She has heard this before.

"A long time ago," Mrs. Puig agrees at once. Still, clearly not long enough. She pats the edges of the serving dish with the hot pads, quieting the fish.

"My husband was not a large man, but he had large needs. He liked to work with the heaviest materials— steel, concrete. Not that he lifted those himself, but he had to motivate his men. He used to say it was like being a football coach, you didn't have to tackle anybody, but you had to convince dumb guys to do it for you."

Simone laughs, although this has been said without

humor, perhaps with reverence. Mrs. Puig shoves at the fish with the spatula. "My husband's voice could carry clear across the site. Although, it was the disappointment of his life he hardly ever got the big jobs, not the really big ones. He'd lose the commission just by a hair's breadth, time after time.

"And then the Department of Transportation," she concludes. She must assume Simone already knows about this, because she makes no move to explain how it was a new government building in Albany where Mr. Puig ran afoul of the building inspectors, was judged liable for a million dollar overrun and began his professional slide. "That's why I had to leave the house in Montauk, I couldn't keep it up after he passed away."

"Perhaps it's just as well. You have more distractions in the city."

"One thing my husband and I had in common," Mrs. Puig says. "We both wanted things to be perfect! But what was perfect for him was not always the same for me." She presses fingertips to her cheekbone. "The things they said about him! In Albany, and after he died. The *obituaries*. I didn't recognize the person they were talking about. You understand? As if I'd been married to somebody quite different—Jekyll and Hyde. " And Simone has a sudden insight into that marriage, the swarthy bender of pipes and caster of concrete, arms outflung—"I want things to be perfect!"—locked in with this little metal-spatter of a woman who is now tearing parsley heads into equal bits and arranging them on each half-moon of potato.

"I was not meant to have these things happen to me," says Mrs. Puig. (*Hester. Mom.*) "I was meant to have a quiet life."

Simone sees the number of poached fish in the years ahead, one after another on platters, as if on a conveyor belt. She sees the hours spent in this kitchen, twisting ice cubes out of a metal tray and filling the tray again (a quintessentially American task), listening to the same complaints, decanting apologetically a gift cheese so ripe that Mrs. Puig's nostrils flare. She shakes this portent from her head.

"I'm so sorry," Simone says.

She is sorry. She remembers what Martin told her once: *in purely evolutionary terms, the only function of memory is prediction.* Her impulse was to protest this— *what about identity, history?*—but she can see that if you don't have any future to speak of, too much past just drags you down. Mrs. P. squares a tea towel on the tiles. Such a mousy way of being in the world. No sense of the Order of Things except in stacking and straightening. Simone makes a quick, implicit vow never to let her vision narrow. *The sea is there! And who shall drain its yield!*

"Well," sighs Mrs. Puig. "Well, that's all water over the dam."

"It seems to me," Simone says, "the gods of Olympus are your perfect example of intermittent reinforcement."

"Explain."

"Well, you never know if Athena or Venus or whoever

is on your side."

They are showing off for Martin's mother, scintillating and arch. There's no harm in it. It's a form of making love. They can send little messages of appreciation, wit, exploring in this public way how their minds entwine, complement, diverge. By comparison with all those rough and tumble meals at the Wombles, the stilted niceties under Mrs. Moxham's gaze, the tension at the Heywoods,' the girl-gossip at Arden House, this is her—no, their—moment to shine.

"You sacrifice your goat and get the seer to read the entrails, and you never know exactly why the god or goddess gives you the winds or the strength in your arm, or whether the same thing will get you the same result next time."

Chewing, chin on hand, he regards her appreciatively. Foreplay is the part of lovemaking at which she's best, so far. It's the banter that arouses her, and the hunger in his gaze. According to *Introduction to Psychoanalysis* she is sexually immature, so when they are in the act, she works at willing her orgasm backwards into her vagina, which would be a tribute to him (Martin, not Freud), but which usually only makes her anxious and stops her coming altogether. Then she fakes, which makes her feel corrupt, which makes her wary of the whole transaction. At the moment she is wary of the beets, their proximity to new linen. She edges around them with her fork and picks at the fish.

"I think you're onto something," Martin says. "So

naturally they have to keep carving up the goats."

Mrs. Puig wears a tentative, attentive smile, as if she understands maternal awe may be required. "Has Martin told you about intermittent reinforcement, Mrs. Puig?" Simone asks. She knows she's being condescending, but she doesn't know how, otherwise, to bridge the territory between her lover and his mother. On their white plates sit the white fish and the white potatoes and mayonnaise and a mound of oozing pickled beets. The contrast is startling, the root more visceral-seeming than the fish.

"It's training the rats, isn't it?"

'Or mice or dogs. If you reward them *every time* for doing something, that isn't as effective as if you just reward now and then. It's an unexpected finding. The frustration leads to doubled effort."

"The only problem with your Greek analogy," Martin says, "is the seer. All that hocus pocus!"

"Yes, I knew you'd say that. But don't you get it?—the seer is the scientist! What is it you do but read the animals' entrails after you've sacrificed them?"

Martin's mouth twitches with irritation, but he cocks his head and throws a hand up. 'Touché."

It's not only showing off. They are also practicing, the way children practice playing house. They are trying out dinner conversation against the time they will entertain colleagues at their own table. Simone leans far over her plate and pokes two small whole beets in her mouth. Thin red tang floods her jaw. She remembers with a jolt that Martin's father shot himself on a white carpet. It comes to her—a preposterous notion—that Mrs. Puig has chosen this color scheme on purpose. She chews without straightening and, still bending over her plate, brings her napkin to her mouth. There's a small flower of brilliant vinegar on the napkin, but her dress is safe.

"There's another problem," Simone admits. "The Gods are always quarreling among themselves. It's as if you were teaching the rat to ring a bell for food, and every time it rang the bell your lab assistant was giving it a shock."

"We don't shock them," Martin says severely. "We use positive reinforcement only."

"Martin," Mrs. Puig asks suddenly, "do you have any use for those old *Hardy Boys*?"

Martin and Simone exchange a rueful glance. Simone says lightly, "You can't be much of a behaviorist if you can't train your *mother*." And bites her tongue.

To his mother Martin says, "I don't get the connection."

"What?"

"Between Hardy Boys and rats. Or bells? Or shocks?"

"I was only saying."

"*I* was only wondering what concatenation you had in mind." Martin describes a mock-professorial spiral in the air. "The *conversational transition*? A logical bridge? Some sop to sequence."

"Only I was going through some boxes, and I was thinking I might give them to the Goodwill."

"What's the matter with you? Those books are practically antiques. Besides." Here he lifts a grin to

Simone that takes her breath away, a look as clear as the passing of an eclipse, "What if I have a boy of my own? You wouldn't want to deprive him, would you?"

Restlessness and joy war in her, a desire to be out of here. To be clattering along a Village street, belting out rhythms, Nickels in May! and then melting into the sweetsome future. So much of life is patience, tight little reins on the imperfect moment, a compromise with the clear sweep of what's to come.

"Have you been mucking around in my room again?" Martin's voice hardens.

"I try to keep it *clean*."

"Just leave it, can't you? I'll clear it out when I have a house to put it in."

A house to put it in, a cottage with a peaked roof, his old tennis rackets, dumbbells, *Hardy Boys* in storage under the beams. What would she put there of her own, if any souvenir of her childhood had survived? All that comes to mind is the string bag her mother used to take to market before the war, a limp nothing-in-itself, but which would magically fill with paper packets, marzipan, beets and turnips with their tops still burgeoning.

Mrs. Puig has taken on her self-belittling air, her *don't-mind-me.* She has a mouthful of fish, and meticulously sets herself to chewing it. When she's done, she says in a tight voice, "You say so, but it's me that has to live with all this *memorabilia.* That coin collection fell all over the closet floor last week."

"What are you talking about?"

"Those Buffalo-whatevers."

"My Indian heads?" says Martin.

"You know what I think? I think there must be rats in the space between the walls."

"There are no rats. It's vibrations from the pipes."

"You say. But Mrs. Delphine has a flea infestation."

"*Non sequitur*, Mother. What did you do with my coins?"

"She had to get the fumigation people in. They taped up all her doors and she had to wash every smidgeon of kitchenware."

"Mrs. Delphine has fleas because of that Pan-Asian yapper. What did you do with my coins?"

"It's just a little dog," Mrs. Puig appeals defensively to Simone. "A Lhasa. Called Paramour."

Simone says, "Maybe Paramour got loose in the walls."

You can feel how unwanted a joke is, how wrong it sits in the souring atmosphere. There must be a scientific explanation for this. People thought radio waves were magic before they could explain them in mathematical terms; some thought the radio itself was a voodoo-box. Some day they will find that anger waves, danger waves, dance in the air in atomic particles called *flupons* or *grideads*. You have sensors in the follicles of your facial hair to read them; they make the air around your eyes feel hot.

"How long do we have to allow to get to the Village?" Simone asks quickly.

"It's not in the Village, it's at Down in the Depths on

Madison."

"Oh!" Simone laughs at herself. "I thought it was a musical!"

"Mike Nichols and Elaine May, the new social satire. They're terrific," he says irritably. "I thought you'd've heard of them."

Lightly, placatingly: "I count on you to keep me *au courant*." But she's disappointed. She'd been hoping for something rousing and romantic. Social satire is a bit of a downer. Martin has the boiled look of somebody stifling anger.

"I thought it was Nickels *in* May!" she says, making a joke of herself. "Would you like me to get the coffee, Mrs. Puig?"

But it doesn't work. Mrs. Puig is rocking her fish knife on the tablecloth. Martin fixes his mother in his sights. "What did you do with the Flying Eagle?"

"I don't know. It took me half the afternoon to stick them back in those cardboard things."

The muscles go rigid in his maxilla, and (like radio waves, inexplicably transferred through the medium of blood or air) the spasm takes up its place in Simone's diaphragm.

"What are *those cardboard things*?"

Mrs. Puig pinches her mouth. "You haven't looked at those coins for years."

"What about: *Official Whitmac Coin Folders*?"

"If you say so." She drops her eyes, smooths the tablecloth over the concrete slab.

"No, I'm serious. Does the term *numismatic* ring a

bell? "

It hurts to see him wax sarcastic—because why, really, should his mother care about his coin collection?—though Simone knows he is operating on some hurt just out of sight, a wound that will not heal, and will not heal.

"Go on, give it a shot. When was the last silver dollar minted? What was on the peace dollar of 1921?"

"It was your hobby, dear. I never claimed it was mine."

"Right. But that's not the point, is it? The point is that my father gave me those coins."

A silence falls. Martin has a vindicated look from which Simone averts her eyes.

"This apartment," Mrs. Puig says in a strangled voice, "this apartment is a...monument to your father."

"Right." He wheels back to Simone, so fiercely that her lungs clench. "Do you get a picture of what it was like growing up with this? The arch nay-sayer of New York, the Queen of Mean—not in the sense of cruel, which would at least have some energy about it—I mean squeezing the life out of anything that gave you pleasure. Never allowed to come in contact with a germ or a lick of sugar or God forbid, a *dog*."

He addresses Simone, not his mother, and she averts her eyes. Her heart pounds hot.

"Do you know I was the only kid in the first grade who came to school in a *tie*? Day after day trying to squash it in my pocket between the sidewalk and the hall; I'd come home, she'd be labeling leftovers, she'd be clipping coupons, she'd be *combing the fringe on the rug*—until Dad threw the damn rugs out altogether. And then got out himself; you can make a wild stab at why."

The mechanism of Mrs. Puig's body is slowing down. A cube of potato fails to reach her mouth, retraces its staccato rhythm to the plate.

Martin leans across to Simone, so near that she feels the heat of his breath and sees the lower row of his bared teeth. "It's very interesting, really, what goes into the formation of such pettiness. It'd make a good research project: round up a hundred and fifty women who spend their days scratching at the gunk around their faucets. Work backwards to figure out what pattern of reinforcement made their minds so goddam fucking *small.*"

He scrapes his chair back, a metal gouging sound on the parquet, and wads his napkin down, striding off toward his old room. Simone reaches out a hand to keep the napkin from unfurling into the beets. There appears not anything so formed as a thought, rather as a swipe of sample color on the folds of cloth, the sudden bright conviction: *I should run.* She can distinguish the place in her stomach where the chewed fish sits, and the vinegar. *Run, run.* And with low clarity she hears her father's voice saying, *"Va t'en. Continue."*

Go away. Go on.

Her breath comes short and burns her throat. She only plays at auguries. She has never understood what people mean by "hearing voices," and she knows this voice is in her head. Still, it has body and heft. It is as recognizable as a voice on a telephone. She thinks of Beckett's tramps: *I can't go on. I will go on,* and as in a dream she calls out without being able to call out (does she expel a breath, a grunt?)—"Ça j'ai fait. J'ai couru et courru. Maintenant je me reste ici." *I've done that. I've run and run. Now I will stop here.*

Mrs. Puig holds her back stiff against the canvas sling, training her gaze brightly on her empty plate, and as if waking Simone sees again the arbitrary grace of the clean-picked bones; a translucent fan, beet juice coagulating in the gelatin. But Martin's temper—it's always aimed at the petty, the ugly. He will never treat her the way he treats his mother. Will he?

"Mrs. Puig," she says. "He doesn't mean it, he's under pressure, trying to teach two labs and carry on his own research. He barks at me too, when he's overtired."

"Oh, no." Mrs. Puig wipes her mouth and looks up with her withered smile. "You see," she says. "for my son you have to *be* somebody. And for him you *are* somebody. And I'm not."

Mrs. Puig has never astonished her before. Who would have guessed the little woman could take her own measure? Simone reaches forward and covers the sinewy hand. "Really...Hester. He's just overworked and overtired."

But she sits amazed—at the insight, the unsuspected self-knowledge. See? Even Mrs. Puig knows he would never, never treat her badly. And there's the implicit compliment: *I am somebody.*

The glamour of Martin's social circle comes into her head: the bohemians who aren't married but have children, the baby faced boy working his way up the ladder at NBC, the Commnist Party member who makes no bones about it. Kuli Moyala from Sierra Leone, dark as Marmite, who moves like Cassandra arrogant among the Greeks. Joyce Glassman, who seemed friendly and modest—but turned out to be Jack Kerouac's girlfriend. Somebody, then.

Simone feels tender toward this stunted person who will be her mother-in-law. She leaves her hand for the moment over the age-spotted, fragile hand, the bones prominent under her own smooth palm. She even dares a gentle stroke, which Mrs. Puig allows. Simone's eyes fall on her own ring finger, where she projects as clear as day the golden circle and its black—gray, really—precious pearl.

It will be all right with Martin. Satire is the thing to mend his mood. Nichols and May!—what foolishness. They will laugh about it later. And about the essentials she is right. Clairvoyant, even. He will ask her tonight. He will be drained of anger, penitent. He will cling to her.

I want everything to be perfect! She is washed over with well-being. She pushes away the doubt. And she wonders how from such unpromising beginnings she herself has arrived at this richly blessed place: a woman with cleavage, and a thesis topic, and the love of a complicated man.

The angry psalms are making a lot of sense right now

by Bethany Lee

And then your storehouses burned down in the night and
you didn't die but came begging
from the ones you'd robbed to fill them
And they fed you, we fed you because
that's. what. we. do. but you looked
when we brought out our food
from where we kept it
and in the night you came back and took it
Took the flour we meant for our children and the oil that
ran out no matter
how we prayed
and we couldn't stop you because
you'd taken the strong ones away
to work in your fields which had been ours until you took
them too and left
the sick behind broken
with no way to walk after
You divided our land
and let your warriors separate us

and some of us didn't notice until it was too late but some
of us have been keening all along
And I know we're all meant to be in this together but you
chose not to be one of us
you thought your hoard could keep you safe but we are
not safe unless we are safe together and we will not be
safe together until
we are willing to be in pain together
and I want to look you in the eyes and say "Does it really
feel safe to be this alone?"
So now here we are
with wheat for one last loaf of bread
and no one here to multiply it for us
and you are saying, "By law that loaf is mine"
even though we all know
you are the one who made the law
that claims this provision
you with the greedy hands and empty eyes
you who gather a double portion
just to keep it away from us
And I don't know how this story ends
It might end with your transformation
or with many needless deaths
and a cloud of grief over all we love but the ending that
scares me most is the one where I am so afraid
I snatch the meal from you
lay it down in the soil where it grew freely and turn our
bread to bricks
for the wall of my own storehouse

Parable of the Painting

by Benjamin Gorman

The education beat in a small town is the way a lot of journalists like me get their start. It's mostly high school football and basketball games, with the occasional controversy when the teachers' union and the school district can't agree on a contract and things get heated. The rest of the time, the board meetings are the worst part of the job. But I will never forget one story I was not allowed to tell at the time. Now that I live far away, I can tell this to you. It feels all the more salient in these dark days.

Pleasanton was a small town which was quietly turning into a bedroom community for the megalopolis growing nearby. It still managed to retain some of its charm through a fealty to its history. Though it didn't have many claims to fame, it could boast that the woman in the famous Alfred Eisensteadt photograph, a dental assistant being kissed by one of the returning sailors on V-J Day in Times Square at the end of World War II, had returned to Pleasanton after the war (without that sailor), married, and had become something of the town matriarch. Her name was Elizabeth Miller when the picture was taken. She passed away in the 90s, but her two sons had become pillars of the community. Their names were Maxwell and Robert Birkshire. Max was one of the leading businessmen in town, owning the bowling alley and the movie theater, though his most profitable businesses were the fast food franchises located across the river in the city. Bob was the pastor of the Methodist church, the largest congregation in Pleasanton. As dictated by the town's size and traditions, these leading figures were obligated to serve either on the city council or the school board, and both had chosen to run for positions on the latter. The only other member of the school board was Mary Patrick, a retired teacher who had earned the love of the town despite her stern demeanor and strict classroom discipline because, after forty years as the only math teacher, she was a unifying presence; everyone had served their time in Mrs. Patrick's classroom.

Now, in addition to sharing parents and a hometown, Max and Bob were alike in many other ways. Max was a parishioner in Bob's church, and Bob frequented Max's bowling alley even more often. But the two men differed in one crucial way, and neither was aware of this distinction because each lacked the knowledge about himself. Bob knew his ability to distinguish colors had been fading, but he was unaware that he'd become completely colorblind. Max had slipped on the ice just a few weeks earlier and cracked his head on the pavement, and while he was being treated for the recurring migraines, no doctor had yet noticed a particular brain damage he'd suffered as a consequence of the fall. Max could no longer identify many shapes.

So the first part of the whole debacle should have been comical. Louise Vandercreek challenged the inclusion of a particular painting which was housed in the glass case outside the art room, and according to the school district's policies, all such challenges had to be brought before the school board. She'd lodged the formal challenge back in November, but then Louise's dog got his snout caught in some chicken wire, and she had to rush him off to the vet's for some stitches, so she couldn't make it to the December meeting to explain her objection. Since the painting had been on the agenda for three weeks and the planned choir recital had been canceled because of all the ice on the roads, the three members of the board decided to move ahead with the objection issue rather than push it off until the next year's board calendar.

Ms. Rappaport, the young and timid new art teacher at Pleasanton High, brought the painting up to the podium covered in a white sheet, set it on top without revealing the image, and leaned over the microphone. Her voice was soft and hesitant, and she had trouble looking up at the three people on the stage, though she made an effort. "Mr. Birkshire. Mrs. Patrick. Rev. Birkshire. This is the painting that's the next item on the agenda. As you know, we had a parent complaint. For obvious privacy reasons, I won't name the student who painted it. I think it displays a great deal of skill, but I admit the content of the painting is a bit controversial. I don't want my own biases to ... um ... color your judgement, so I will just show you the painting and let you decide." Then, with a flourish that contradicted her mousey voice, Ms. Rappaport whipped the sheet off the painting.

The image under the sheet was not merely composed of a painting. It was a blown up image of Alfred Eisensteadt's famous black and white photograph, with colored paint applied on top. Done with extreme care to match the shades of gray, the high school artist had matched very dark reds and greens to the darkest parts of the painting, and very light reds and greens to the lightest parts, but these colors were applied selectively along the angle of the young Elizabeth Birkshire Miller's angled body and the crook of the sailor's arm which held her head, and the shape of the colored portion was quite obviously that of an erect, veiny, gigantic penis. The artist (everyone at school knew it was that goth girl, Judith Molleur) had not done this by accident. She was attempting to comment on the fact that the image, long presented as an icon of celebration and patriotism, was in fact a depiction of sexual assault. This was a very fair critique; Eisensteadt and the sailor (whose identity is still disputed to this day because multiple men proudly claim to be the one in the picture) set up the image and chose a total stranger for the sailor to kiss. Eisensteadt chose Elizabeth because she was pretty and happened to be wearing white, and he knew that would make for a striking contrast. Elizabeth was not consulted in any way. The sailor simply ran up, grabbed her, kissed her, Eisensteadt snapped the picture, and then the men ran off. Elizabeth found herself on magazine covers and in history books being kissed by a total stranger, only the people of Pleasanton knew or cared, and they considered it an honor. Her opinion of the whole affair was never quite clear. Was she merely being humble when asked about it? Was she ashamed? Was she just tired of the attention? She took that secret to her grave. But Judith Molleur saw the image through modern eyes and recognized it for what it was, and she wanted the rest of the school to see it her way, so she chose the vivid reds and greens for her giant penis painting.

Of course, that's not what the Birkshire brothers saw at all. Bob, by virtue of his colorblindness, saw an almost perfect replica of the famous photograph, with just enough brushstrokes that he could tell it was painted. Max, on the other hand, saw a bright splash of red and green against a mottled grey background in some shape he couldn't identify, a piece of modern art with a possible Christmas theme. And they might have cleared up their misconceptions quickly enough had the chair of the board, Mrs. Patrick, not spoken first.

She leaned toward her microphone and then shot warning glances at the men on either side of her, the same glare she'd used in her math classes to preempt students she knew were about to speak out of turn.

"Alright, before we discuss this, I have to remind everyone that this conversation is on the record in an open session. We have a number of bylaws that need to be adhered to as we discuss this matter. First of all, there are laws about student privacy to be considered, so we cannot say anything that might reveal the identity of the artist, so I'll just warn you to be careful about that. Secondly, because of the picture's content, we may have some conflicts of interest to keep in mind, so let's not be too specific about *who* is in the painting. Thirdly, because of the painting's content and our rules about obscenity, we need to be very careful not to mention exactly *what* is in the painting. I mean," she chortled a bit, a dry raspy sound that reminded everyone schools used to allow smoking in the teachers' lounges, "we all know what we're looking at. But we're not going to talk about that." There was some chuckling from a few members of the assembled audience who had heard about the painting and had come for the show, but because the podium was in the middle of the room and the painting faced the school board, most of the people there that night couldn't see the painting and didn't get Mrs. Patrick's joke. "Okay," she continued, "I'm going to move that we should not allow the painting to be displayed at the school. Do I have a second?"

Neither man spoke. She looked back and forth. "Bob? Max? Either of you want to second my motion?"

Bob leaned back in his chair. "Look, I know it's not the usual Robert's Rules of Order, but I think we should debate this a bit before we move forward on this. And I don't know quite how to debate it without talking about all the things we're not allowed to talk about, so I'm just going to say it: I think the painting is great, and I think we should keep it on display."

"Really?" Mrs. Patrick asked, sincerely surprised.

"Well, I don't want to cross any lines here, but I feel a strong personal connection to this painting. Beyond that, I think it says something important to the kids about our town of Pleasanton and its history, and I don't see why we should hide that."

Mrs. Patrick managed to keep her mouth from hanging open. Had the town's most prominent man of the cloth just made a reference to the size of his ... loins, in front of God and everybody? She couldn't help but swivel in slow motion to get support from Max.

Max shrugged. "Now, I see it differently. I think we should keep it up there, too, but not because of any historical reason and certainly not because of any personal connection. Frankly, I don't see myself in this painting at all. I just think it's important that the kids be allowed to express themselves in these new ways. They're the future, and we don't want our traditional views of things to be limiting what they can do. I'm just not comfortable with that kind of censorship in the name of tradition. So I say leave it up and let the kids do their thing."

Now Mrs. Patrick's mouth did hang open. Had the town's leading businessman just shared something about his own feelings about his ... anatomical inadequacies on the record in an open session of the school board meeting? Or was that a comment about his parentage. Max looked so much like Bob, and they both resembled their mother in such striking ways, that she'd never even considered the possibility he wasn't a blood relative. But maybe they'd had some falling out she didn't know about.

Bob took offense for a different reason. How could his brother deny the historical importance of this painting of their mother? "Look, Max, I know you aren't quite as traditional as some of us, but you have to admit this has deep, deep meaning for our family. I find this painting really penetrating, like to my soul, Max. You understand that, right?"

"Hey," Max said, a bit more sharply, "I don't appreciate your condescending tone, Bob. Of course I can see why this might have some holiday significance to you, and it might even touch you on a spiritual level, but to me it's about freedom and energy and ... yeah, I'll say it. It's about love, Bob. Not in some pious church way, but in a secular, modern way. And it's a public school, so that seems totally appropriate to me."

Bob shook his head. "See? There you go. You go off to the city and get all these big ideas that secularism is the way to go and we can forget all about our history and traditions. And that's what's wrong with this country, Max. It's people like you, losing touch with their roots."

Max leaned over his mic. "Something is wrong with this country alright. We've got Mrs. Patrick here who wants to censor things that are outside her preconceived notions of what art should look like, and then you, the minister, wanting to make everything about your religious devotion to the past, and I've got news for you, Bob. That? That right there?" He pointed angrily at the painting. "That's not about the past, okay? That's about the future. That's about progress."

Bob threw his hands up. "That doesn't even make any sense! You want to make everything about progress and the future, and normally I let you go about your businesses and don't make a fuss, but this? This is one thing that's cut and dried. This is about tradition. And if we can't agree on that, I don't know what comes next. Everything is subjective now? Postmodern? Sometimes a cigar is just a cigar, and why can't we be happy with this big ol' cigar in our mouths?"

All the laughter in the room had vanished. Mrs. Patrick had been swinging her head back and forth, but now she fixed it straight ahead, and only her eyes, opened as wide as they could go, ping-ponged as the men spoke.

"Yeah, I see what you're doing there. I'm the cigar smoking capitalist, right? One minute I'm too liberal because I like things that are new and creative, so I'm a commie socialist, and the next minute I'm some capitalist pig because you chose to work for a church instead of starting your own businesses. Jesus Christ, Bob, there's no winning with you!"

"Hey! You may not care about our family anymore, but don't you take the Lord's name in vain in front of me or I swear to God I will come over this table and beat your ass!"

Mrs. Patrick snatched up the gavel, at first to protect it from the wobbling table, then to use it to protect herself, and then, remembering she could do so, to end the meeting. She hammered it down eight times, at least five more than were necessary, before she caught herself and calmly announced the brief recess that would turn out to be the end of the meeting since, five minutes later, they no longer had a quorum, both men having left.

And this whole fiasco might have blown over, if not for what happened the next week. One of the items that had been further down on the agenda was an urgent request from the custodial staff at Pleasanton Elementary for an emergency purchase of salt. They hadn't accounted for the extra icy winter hitting so early (though Max's head had already felt its effects violently), and they were running low. The district could easily have afforded the salt, but it required school board action to move money from the general fund to the maintenance fund. This could even have been done with a few phone calls the next day, but the brothers refused to speak with each other. So on Monday, when two children and a parent fell in the school parking lot and little Matty Parks broke his wrist in two places, the town went into an uproar. They called the paper wanting answers, and I had a story written about the board meeting which would have cleared up a lot of the confusion, but Mrs. Patrick, after refusing to comment to me on the record, had called my editor and reminded him that if they ever wanted to get a story about anything educational printed with district help in the pages of the *Pleasanton Herald,* he would make sure the story abided by the same strictures as the board members and not describe anything that might identify the student or include any references to the obscene nature of the painting. My editor went at my story with his red pen, and pretty soon it made almost no sense. But that wasn't enough for Mrs. Patrick. My editor showed her the story before he ran it, and she was furious with the depiction of the board in chaos, so she hopped online and told everyone that they couldn't trust the *Pleasanton Herald* or me personally, that we were liars and as biased as the least ethical examples of what passed for journalists in the mainstream media, and that if people wanted the real story, they should listen to the people who had been in attendance and not some young reporter who lived across the river and commuted into Pleasanton to make fun of them for being provincial yokels.

The angry citizens of Pleasanton took her advice and privately interviewed the few people who had been at the meeting, most of whom had never seen the painting under discussion. These people, depending on their biases, told elaborate stories of the valiant and moral Max defending himself and the town from the cowardly and evil Bob, or vice versa. Most people initially fell into camps based on which of the two brothers they'd already liked better, and in days the painting itself was forgotten. The debate became about secularism vs. religiosity or censorship vs. first amendment rights or progress vs. tradition or, inexplicably, guns and abortion. This shift away from the painting was exacerbated by a habit of the citizens of Pleasanton; whenever they were confronted with an argument, it was considered socially acceptable to say, "Oh yeah? Well what about…" and then bring up some other, completely unrelated grievance.

Consequently, rather than have a single debate about an issue, people tended to have wide ranging gripe fests that were mostly about tallying hypocrisy points. Then, when these debates became uncomfortable, people would try to find common ground by saying Max and Bob were politicians and therefore equally untrustworthy, and that both sides were equally at fault. By the next summer, there were rumblings of recall efforts, and both brothers announced they were not running again, so, in addition to losing a lot of their standing in the community and what had previously been a tight sibling bond, they also lost their positions on the school board and were replaced by people who were far less competent except when it came to their key campaign promises to make damned sure the district was always well stocked on salt. People stopped coming to Bob's church because they had heard he was some kind of villain. Others stopped going to Max's bowling alley and movie theater. While the brothers weathered these financial hits, those people lost their faith communities and their bowling leagues and their date nights next to their neighbors. The whole town of Pleasanton was diminished.

To be honest, I'm not sure my story would have made a whole lot of difference after that initial weekend. Once Mrs. Patrick told everyone not to believe the *Pleasanton*

Herald, they were doomed, and even learning the true story wouldn't have mattered all that much. Part of the both-sides impulse that turned the town on Max and Bob also manifested in their reaction to every other story put out by the paper, and I've heard that went on even after I moved away. Somehow the people of Pleasanton felt that it was their civic responsibility to believe a version of events which fell at the perfect halfway point between whichever two stories they heard, as though the most correct understanding is the middle-est, even if it's halfway between the true account and a lie.

I'm reminded of this sometimes when I hear people use some of the same buzzwords I jotted down as Bob and Max shouted at each other. It would be nice if we could talk about Bob's value of history, as long as we could include Judith Molluer's recognition that we have a lot in our past that is ugly and needs to be reckoned with. It would be nice if we could talk about Max's desire for progress and freedom without being scared that we'll step on Bob's love of his religious tradition. There are parts of the painting we can't see alone. But let's not both-sides this. Max and Bob and the people of Pleasanton weren't undone by the differing values of the brothers. The town was prohibited from having one shared, true story, and they chose to abide by that prohibition. I'm not some perfect, impartial arbiter of right and wrong. I'm just a woman doing her best to tell the story accurately. And if we don't agree to hear each other's stories and try to figure out the truth, we're left alone, locking ourselves out of our churches and bowling alleys and movie theaters, refusing to talk to our brothers, and making kids like little Matty Parks suffer for it.

Now some people will try to make peace in Pleasanton by saying, "Let's not blame anyone. Not Max. Not Bob. It's all in the past anyway. No one is to blame." But they're wrong. Mrs. Patrick is to blame, and learning that is the key to understanding what is currently happening in Pleasanton.

When we aren't allowed to talk about the painting in front of our own eyes, and when we refuse to believe the people who can see more than we do, it has consequences.

Scorched Earth

by Zack Dye

"Are you ready for this Burn? The fire department will be here in just a little bit to set the perimeter fires," Amber said.

"I know. I need a little more time," Donovan said. "But I'll be ready when they get here." He peeled the long, black hair back from his tanned, white face. He looked at his wife of sixteen years and thought of the many Burns they had shared before, even before they were married, when they were young and frivolously in love. Now they had three kids and the vineyard. This year was especially challenging because it was a Burn year, when they had to not only burn down the brush around the farm but the vines themselves.

"When are we able to replant?"

"Amber.. Honey," Donovan offered a bit haltingly, I'm trying to wrap up a few more things in the winery before we get out of here."

"Sorry, I just want to know when we're able to come back and plant again."

"Well, I got the express grow vines coming in four weeks. So really, we should be able to get back by then to plant. Sometime just after Christmas, I guess."

"They just take six months to mature right? Last time you got the wrong ones and it took an extra year."

"Oh my god! How many times do I have to apologize for that? They were cheaper. And you're right, I didn't look carefully that time. It was the first time I ordered by myself without your dad's help. But that's why I need this extra time... that's why I can't really have you bothering me right now!"

"I don't think I'm bothering you. I'm just trying to make sure you don't screw it up again."

"Screw it up agai..." Donovan cut himself off. He knew better than to keep arguing. So he just packed up the screen-pad he was using for his online ordering. Then he went back out to the winery. But he certainly wanted to try and have the last word, so he made sure to slam the door as he walked back outside to the other building.

"We have two hours!" Amber yelled after him. Donovan heard her managing the last word again. And he also knew all of the details too. Yet here they were having another fight. They were arguing over the same particulars; the same points of stress.

Amber stormed back into the house. Music was blasting from behind the door to their recalcitrant daughter Meredith's room — loud beats and crooning falsesetto. "Neo doo-wop for the hormone laden teenage soul. A human staple," Amber thought to herself before going in to parent her eldest.

Amber knocked on the door once without answer. She pushed it open after that, her patience worn thin. "Mom!"

"We need to get out of here. Did you get everything you need ready for the next month?"

"I'm getting dressed!" Meredith stammered as she darted into her bathroom taking her phone with her. The door closed behind her, "I'm talking to Petra about everything before we leave!" she barked back through the door. Amber just turned around and walked out. She didn't have the energy to double check what she was packing and if Meredith would be ready in time. Her fifteen year old daughter was darling and intelligent but right now all she could think about was how absent minded she was, worried only about her two hobbies: talking to friends and meeting cute boys online.

The cacophony of the house hallway was driving her mad. She strode down the hall to check on their eleven year old twins Jacob and James. They exhausted her and Donovan at every turn, since they were heavily involved in every community activity: indoor baseball, soccer, community theater, school dance recitals, and their own rock band. As she got to their door, she could hear the discordant playing of classic hits from ancient bands from over a hundred years ago. Distorted guitar slowly squeaked through their door. The two boys were into oldies like Nirvana and Pearl Jam, the kind of music Donovan and Amber's great, great grandparents had listened to.

"Stop playing music," she commanded as she entered their room not even bothering to knock and looking past the clothes strewn about the room or the toys covering the floor. They both were still her babies and she felt no inclination to respect their oncoming adolescence the way she did with Meredith.

"But moooommmm!" the two howled in unison as they stopped hitting the drums and strings of the electric guitar their grandfather Leonard had bought them two Christmases ago before he passed.

"You need to be ready in 15 minutes. I see your bags are packed. Double check them, pick this room as best you can in 10 minutes and then take everything you're bringing out to the car. You have the same instruments..."

"You know those aren't as good as the ones from Gran-"

Continuing where she left off, "...same instruments at grandma and grandpa's in California. You can keep practicing there. I've had it up to here today, though. Stop playing around and get ready to go." She bothered with no more niceties at this point. The Burn was coming; she was struggling to get everyone ready. She still had to get her mother wheeled out to the car and settled in the back before they drove her into downtown Yuma for a month-long stay at an assisted living facility. This chore she disliked most of all because she envied the continence of Donovan's parents, still able-bodied and energetic in their lives out by the coast. Instead she had to mind her husband, her children and her mom for whom she nursed and cared.

During the burn of 2125, Alice had tried to go back to get one of the dogs they had forgotten in a rush to leave. She couldn't find the dog and she lost track of where she was. She was trapped in the blaze that the firefighters had started. When the firefighters found her they were tamping down the Burn. She was barely breathing, comatose from excessive smoke inhalation. After six weeks in a coma she opened her eyes but she was never the same. She couldn't talk nor could she walk by herself, confined to a chair. She recognized only Amber and her husband Leonard. So, Alice also lived with Donovan and Amber. As painful as this was, Amber and Leonard decided it was best to keep her close and care for her. Since Leonard had died somewhat recently and Alice's condition subsequently worsened further, this had become yet another point of stress.

The wine glass was never empty in front of Amber. The bartender in the restaurant downtown knew to never let it get empty. Yuma had always been a western town, but no one thought it would ever be a Mecca for grape growing. "That's the end of the bottle. You wanna keep drinking your own?," the bartender asked Amber.

"No, give me something different. I'm tired of my white shit. I'll pay for it," Amber replied.

"I got a California neo-red. It's a pinot and merlot blend."

"Jesus. A hundred years ago they'd never put those

grapes together. But it is what is. Give it to me... I mean, is it good?"

"Yeah it's good. Like you said, it ain't that white shit... no offense Amber."

"Nah. None taken."

"Another Wednesday, huh, Ms. Smith-Clouds?" *Amber usually came in on Wednesday nights.*

"Another Wednesday," she sighed. The middle of the week is when she got a moment to herself. The kids didn't have activities, so they just wanted to stay in their rooms and play after dinner or talk to friends online. Donovan and her dad always had lots of work to do in the winery anyways: paperwork and calculations among other things. In addition to that she and Donovan had a home equity line of credit to accompany their mortgage for the house built among the vines there, the loan decreasing painfully slowly as they managed their debts and family obligations. Even though the winery was profitable, managing the money and the always fluctuating inputs made Donovan a little unpleasant sometimes: "I just can't do math when people are around," Donovan said. He'd said this since college where he majored in Finance. But with his family always around he seemed to say it all the time when he had to do paperwork.

"Donovan makes you come down here?"

"No, no. I want to come here. He makes me leave the house so I don't kill him, my parents or *any* of our children," she said back to the barkeep who just chuckled and uncorked a bottle.

"Wine making is hard work. That's why I just pour it."

"Listening to me moan and groan about my family seems like hard work to me. I mean, my husband won't do it. He basically is making you do it." She set her payment chip on the bar and motioned for him to charge her for whatever the cost might be.

"You're not alone, if that helps. People are in here all night staying away from the shit that makes them crazy."

"Life!... I mean, it's like the whole thing makes me crazy. I get no time to myself. I don't feel like I get to make any mistakes. And fuck, I feel like all I do is make mistakes. I yelled at my daughter today because she got a bad score on a math review at school. I fucking hate math. I *can't* do it. Like I just said, I make my dad and husband do all that shit, ordering, bills, that crap. But I felt like getting a bad review at school... she needed to be disciplined — that's what my mom did at least. I don't know. She's only ten. Still my baby girl, right?... I just don't know — we're all just hypocrites, I guess," she tapped the glass letting him know she was ready for him to fill her glass again.

"We sure ain't perfect, that's for damn sure," the bartender agreed as he grabbed her chip and went to scan it on the register.

After a couple more glasses of wine, another local came over and sat down next to her. "You ain't drinking your own tonight?," he asked.

"I don't know what I'm doing. Mom's still crazy. Kids don't care about anything. My husband just spends all his time doing paperwork."

"Sounds lonely out at the farm."

"Do I know you?" she asked.

"Yeah. I work over at the res. I've seen you here before. We're both Native. I mean, we're cut from the same cloth, if you know what I mean."

"Just because we're Native?" Amber was of Navajo descent and her family had property near the Gila River which they'd had since white men came and decided that white men should own property. Before, it all belonged to her ancestors but now she had her plot. But only in the last sixty years had the property become useful for agriculture and especially grape growing and her family did what they could to take advantage of it.

The tropical storms that came off the Pacific Ocean and the Sea of Cortez had increased in frequency since the start of the 21st century. The land had much more rain and was much more fertile than the previous millenium. But it was also still quite arid as well. Sometime in the early 21st century Amber's great, great grandfather had taken a trip to Italy and was convinced the newly moistened landscape of the Southwest American desert would lend itself to growing and making Italian style wines because of the similar climates. He decided on growing perera grapes and he converted 20 acres of family land into a perera vineyard. Ultimately, this had been a great decision as the varietal grew quite successfully over the years.

"No, we're both here drinking too much. That's the cloth we're cut from tonight. Sure we're Native, yes," the man said and she chuckled in response. "I've seen you around. I'm Dark Mountain... e'rybody just calls me Monty."

"Ah yeah. I heard that name around." She was exhausted by the end of the day. She couldn't exert any extra information on some local Native with a half-spun yarn of cleverness. The internal thoughts of home beat and her slowly inebriating mind. Her mom's condition made her feel awful. Watching how her father worked the land — now watching Donovan struggle with her family's land too — made her sad. The children and all the work they required made her feel awful too. Ultimately, she wasn't interested in his obvious come-ons.

"You know this is in our genes, right?"

"What, drinking?" Monty nodded when she asked this. "Well yeah, but I mean you can't blame your whole life on genetics."

"I'm not saying it's a problem for us. I'm just saying, well you know we're not from Africa like white folks or black folks. It's that 9-repeat allele. We got a different gene. We been on this land for a long time."

"What allellll?" Amber slurred the "L". She lifted her drunken eyes to his, "I mean, what're you talking about. What's your point?"

"Folks like us are special. When's the last time you looked in the mirror? You're special. Your family owns the winery. You've been here hundreds of years. You're special — I."

"I told you. I'm married," she offered forcibly but through a nervous giggle. Looking at Monty's brown face and long black braids, he was handsome. Although, he looked like any weathered and worn man with soft eyes and weathered face; of average height.

"I'm just gonna buy you another couple drinks. This has nothing to do with you being married. We're all in this together. We're family and even after getting these last seven hundred plus years of Americans and white people, all we've really got are ourselves. You know Native Americans are more closely related to each other than to any other existing Asian populations, except those that live at the very edge of the Bering Strait." She was drunk and knew she wanted another couple drinks, especially tonight. Monty's warm eyes welcomed her. She continued to open up about all these frustrations. They talked deep into the evening until another bottle of wine was empty. Her eyes lost that glow but filled with a longing and loneliness that only people deep in a drunk can have. She didn't know what she wanted except to not want; to not feel; to stop it all for just a little bit.

When she woke up the next morning her watch had over two dozen missed calls and messages from Donovan. She had a splitting headache and no clothes on. When she finally reoriented herself she saw her clothes on a chair in the corner. She got out of bed and went to put them on. She didn't even respond to the questions that came from Dark Mountain in the bed. She hurried out of the house and ordered a car to get her home as quickly as possible.

  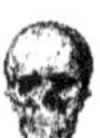

"You've got everything you need?"

"I do. We cleared the house of valuables. You're going to tent it though, right?" Donovan asked as the fireman looked back at the vineyard and surrounding foliage.

"Yeah, just like five years ago."

The Arizona legislature decided that all land should be burned every five years in 2096. Global warming had made the Arizona desert even hotter. But at the time it was the increasing humidity that made the land even more susceptible to fire. The land was more lush, the botany changed and spread rapidly. More plants grew and then dried in those conditions, undergrowth building on undergrowth because the increasingly warm waters of the Pacific let southern storms push more frequently up through Southern California and across the Gila Mountains in the spring and summer to nourish all that plant life.

"I don't really remember, that was a tough time for me. We were going through a tough time around here. Family stuff, you know?" In other communities the intimacy of the conversation might have been awkward but in this small farming community, the local firefighters and other civil servants worked closely with the locals. Suffice to say, this was not the first time Donovan had met this firefighter.

"Sure, sure. Ok, yeah. Everything should be fine. We'll make sure the house and winery are fine — all the structures. We're gonna take the fire up to within one hundred yards of the house. We did the neighbors on each side last year, we haven't had any issues."

Donovan nodded, "I saw. It looks good from what I can see so far this year, for sure."

"Should be a piece of cake. You're ready to replant? Because we'll compost and layer the ash. Then it's ready to plow under, help the soil and such per the ag. department specs."

"Perfect. Yeah, I got the new vines coming in a month. So we're ready for when we're able to come back."

"Where you going?"

"We're going to my folks. We went there last time. They have a nice house out in L.A. It's nice in winter time and the kids love the beach... the kids. They're all so old this time around. Anyway, yeah, we're heading out there."

"Sounds nice. Alright, well, once you're gone in a little bit we'll start getting ready to burn it all down."

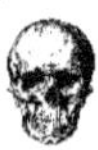

The first time Donovan and the kids went to Los Angeles there was almost no mention of their mother. Amber was certainly an afterthought for Donovan. When she came home that "morning after" he was already too angry to even discuss things. Amber was disheveled and raced directly in to check on Alice. Alice hadn't quite woken up at the time and Amber, after peeking in on her mother, took a quick shower and came out to the kitchen.

The kids loved being with their grandparents in the hot Southern California heat with the pool and the park nearby. It was just right for them at that age. Mornings of cereal with grandpa followed middays spent poolside. In the afternoon Donovan would take them to the park. They ran around yelling after him: "Daddy, daddy! Watch me. Can you see this?"

He would look up coolly and stare in their direction while they jumped from a jungle gym or elevated themselves higher on a swing. He tried to find joy in their simple musings, their running about in the open space joyfully. With Amber having come home "that morning" a few days (or was it weeks?.. some time back, anyway) Donovan could find very little enjoyment in his kids.

As it was, marriage was a concept that frustrated him. Before Amber and Donovan married, life was marvelously frivolous. He looked at Meredith, conceived after a weekend of drunken bliss. Donovan and Amber had gone to a friend's wedding in Seattle for the weekend and amidst the drinking, pomp and romance they found enough moments to indiscriminately have intercourse and some five weeks later Amber was late. Back at home on the Gila River they were discretely celebrating the arrival of their first child, something they had talked about since early on in their relationship.

"Dad, we miss mom," Jimmy came over and said as Jake walked quickly behind him

"I don't give a shit."

"DAD! That's a bad word," the five year olds said in unison.

Donovan immediately felt terrible, "I know. I know. I mean, we can't do anything about it right now. Are you done playing?"

"Yeah, we're done," Jake said.

"Are you mad at Mommy?" Jimmy asked.

"No, I'm not mad. We just needed to come see your grandparents. You get to see grandpa Leonard all the time," he lied to them. He was so hurt at what Amber had done. He reflected on how when she got home "that morning" she couldn't talk to him. By the time they were able to talk about her absence she admitted that she didn't remember the night before. She insisted over and over again that she didn't intentionally do anything wrong. He stood there in front of his kids replaying the whole sequence quietly in his own mind:

"Intentionally?" He shouted back in question form, Amber shrinking in shame. But there was no going back. "If you didn't drink so much you wouldn't have done anything unintentional!" He shot at a glare at her.

Her soul retreated but her anger seethed, "You have no right to stand there and judge!"

"Don't I? This is pointless. I can't keep an eye on the vineyard and the kids and you!"

"On me?" the argument was in full bloom, "I shuttle the kids around. You follow my father around like a lost puppy. I take care of Mom. I do the chores. 200 years on from the feminist movement and I'm still your maid taking care of you like your mother. Who cares whose bed I woke up in and whatever his name was." As the words came out, she instantly regretted them. She had admitted the truth but that was not her intention. At least whatever lie existed was now over. Nonetheless, she felt awful, physically and otherwise.

"Well, are you going to go out and help your dad with all the work out there?" This was phrased as a question but it was certainly an accusation.

"So what if I drink now and again?"

"You don't even know what happened last night but you woke up in a strange man's bed?" This was not a question though, and she cringed further at the truth. The pain between them was stinging. He had a fury in his eyes. She did not feel unsafe but she felt unloved.

In those moments she questioned everything. Did she love him? Did she even want this life? What was the point of their time together if they were to spend it loathing one another. The resentment built inside of her and before the tears burst she yelled, "Well, maybe you're not man enough for this family." Then she left the room slamming each door in all the doorways through which she passed as she stormed away from him. Donovan was left standing there in the middle of the kitchen.

He stood on the edge of the Los Angeles playground much like he had in that kitchen a few weeks earlier. He was close to his family in terms of physical proximity but he was as far away as he could ever be in terms of emotional attachment. He was a white man who had married into a Native family. He was always looking in from the outside and he never felt it more than he did right now. He cursed the generations of Amber's family that came before him. He let epithets of red skin and scalped ghosts race across the front of his mind. He looked at his children and they seemed foreign to him as if they might leave at a whim and forget he ever tried to be their father.

This emasculation pulled hard at all his insecurities. He burned to the core of his heart and felt the heat extend from the middle of his body to each extremity, the fury and embarrassment tingling each finger and toe as he tried to find compassion in himself. He hunted the barren desert of his body for an emotion of concern and love, something that might bind him to this land, this moment, this family that stood right there in front of him. He stood there for what seemed like years.

"Dad?" The voice came from Meredith. "Dad, Jake and Jimmy are right. You look mad. Are you ok?"

He came back to attention, startled from his prison of immobility and lifted up by his own resentments. What, in fact, were they playing at? What was this game of love and marriage between Amber and him and why was it so important? he asked himself. Wouldn't it be easier to disappear into any other world beyond, to exist alone and to fret only at the simple fears of having enough to eat and staying warm on colder nights? The rhetorical questions built until he was shaken loose again by Meredith's hand.

"Dad, I'm only ten. I'm young. But you look hurt. The ancestors tell me when you people are hurt."

"The ancestors? What are you talking about?! Just mind your ow..."

She cut him off before he said more things he knew he would regret, "Dad, when Mom takes me down to the

Res. there's an old quote on one of the walls. I always read it because Mom says that's how I will know her mom. That's the best way to know shima-sani, 'Walking, I am listening to a deeper way. Suddenly all my ancestors are behind me. Be still, they say. Watch and listen. You are the result of the love of thousands.'" His spirit fell silent. "Daddy, I am watching. You are hurt. But I know this because I am the result of your love and the love of thousands."

A tear came to his eye and his heart cried a thousand more hot tears inside from being bent, torn and shredded by the stress of life, just like a rock that finally bursts from the water frozen deeply inside of it, the soft water a forceful cudgel against the hardest stone. Meredith took her dad's hand and they started to walk back to his parents' house.

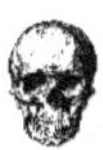

Crops thrived in that Southwestern sunshine and fiery heat. But those dry Augusts, Septembers and Octobers would eventually turn the forest and foliage undergrowth into a tinderbox. As the population grew and farming expanded in the area, humans used the scorched desert forests to nourish crops. Still, the wildfires were most consistent yet unpredictable. Worse, Southwestern air would fill with smoke turning the skies of Albuquerque, Santa Fe, Dallas and Houston a fearful crimson. Finally, the state legislature knew they had to take action.

In the early 2090s science developed mutated strains of plants that could produce a yield within months. This changed the argument the legislature had against intentional burns. Because the vineyards and orchards that were producing great quality grapes, pears, plums, apples and peaches could be razed by fire and return to full production in the harvest following a burn year, the revolutionary tactic to combat the fires began in earnest.

That was when crop burns became the norm. AZ-bill 2098–431b3, Scorched Earth insisted that every five years, all land in certain areas zoned for farming needed to burn and every five years firefighters of the Fire Control Department were required to go through a specified area and do a controlled burn to keep the brush under control.

Because of this requirement, smokey skies would collect and then dissipate every December. Still, there were no uncontrolled burns or wildfires in Arizona any more. The land wasn't ever overgrown and the increase in safety and supervision allowed the farmers to operate with far more certainty. Insurance prices fell which kept operating costs lower as well. With the state using their taxes to fund these projects, the state was able to count on consistent revenue from more consistent yields. The air was healthier and the communities were able to live in better harmony.

Each farm marked their calendars for their "Burning December," as they were more colloquially called. Just prior to a farm's Burning December the dead trees that surround the property are assessed and collected. New trees and vines are ordered for planting in January.

Families move away for some time and trust their land to their firefighters who would burn all the growth but protect all the existing structures. Then, after the smoke clears and the ash settles across the farmland, farmers come back and start again.

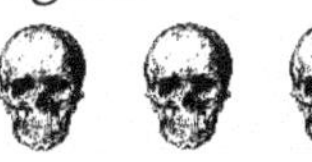

Because of the affair with Monty, Amber ultimately had an abortion. Worse, the way things were progressing between her and Donovan, there seemed almost no way to reconcile. As Donovan hid in California with the kids, Amber stayed at home with the vineyard and her mother, for whom she still had to care. She spent solitary days going over the pain of her infidelity, the pain of caring for an ill parent, the pain of missing her kids, and the pain she felt watching her father struggle to keep it all together while Donovan was gone. She internalized much of the frustration as her being entirely her own fault.

One day she sat there reading aloud to her mother since the doctors said it helped Alice keep in touch with the world around her; keeping her from any accelerated drifting into the afterworld. Even the local "medicine woman" had told her as much when she had visited the res a few weeks prior. As she came to the end of a paragraph, Alice suddenly spoke. "A fight is going on inside me," she said. "It is a terrible fight and it is between two wolves. One is evil — he is anger, envy, sorrow, regret, greed, arrogance, self-pity, resentment... that wolf is my death. "The other is life — she is joy, peace, love, hope, serenity, humility, kindness, benevolence, empathy, generosity, truth, compassion, and faith."

"Mom?" Amber's eyes filled with tears.

"Dear, I am here. I am always here. Please keep reading. I do love it so."

"But Mom, I feel this same fight right now. And the wolves are tearing at each other. My children are gone, my husband is gone, and you are..."

"My dear, I am not gone. Even when I am not here, I will never be gone."

"I am rotting inside, Mother."

"Then you know which wolf is winning. The fight goes on inside you and inside every other person, too. I promise you that it goes on with Donovan as we speak. The world is alight and hurting, the fight is all around us."

Amber paused briefly and then asked, "Which wolf will win?"

Alice looked out the window into the distance, past the pages of the book and into the wooded field beyond the vineyard, that wooded field that 200 years before could not have grown there. The silence was almost deafening to Amber as she awaited her mother's response. It finally came, "The one you feed."

Then the room was silent and Alice was seemingly gone from this conscious world again. The stare continued after the light left her eyes, the brief shining lucidity that brought the histories of her family into the room just moments before. She looked out the same window and saw one of the nighthawk owls still native to the area gliding out of view. Although they're a nocturnal bird normally unseen at this time of the afternoon, Amber wondered if the bird had come to take her mother with her and into the skies.

Donovan and Amber drove the family back out again. Meredith had forgotten her purse. The purse had one of her four entertainment devices in it along with a wallet and a variety of makeup. Meredith begged for these seemingly insignificant keepsakes that were, to a teenager, so terribly important. She swore she would "have to have" these before going to her grandparents for a month. Although trivial to her parents and of absolutely no significance to her younger brothers, the family darted back looking at the clock in hopes of getting to the house before it was sealed by the flame retardant tent and the fires had been set. They drove in against the scenic backdrop of the wooded hills.

"How did you get ten minutes without using *that* phone?... Amber said sarcastically to her daughter, "You know what? I don't care. Let's just get it."

"You forget things all the time," Meredith said back to her mother.

"Mer, this is absolutely not the ti..." Donovan put his hand on Amber's leg and pressed lovingly into the flesh of her knee to cut her off. The two looked at each other as the years of pain and joy swirled above them like distant, ominous storm clouds. They would not burst now, they might not burst at all, but they filled the gaze between them like lightning on the horizon. Amber choked down the rest of her thought and tried again, "I gotta say, 10 minutes without your phone is a record. I'm proud of you," she offered with sincerity, "When we get there your dad will see if we can go back in. You know where you left it?"

"It's on the bathroom *sink*," she said with the impatience of all teenagers talking to their parents

"Of course it is," Donovan whispered to his wife and she smiled. Fending off the responsibilities of the fires was so stressful it felt good, cathartic even, to share a smile between them. Donovan pulled up to the gate where the firefighter from before stood talking into his device, "We forgot her purse," he said motioning to Meredith in the back seat and implying that it was of great, great importance.

The firefighter chuckled. "We've got one car coming back," he said into his watch-device.

"Roger that. One car back," came the voice in the other end.

"The tent is the last thing we put up since the fire usually starts furthest away from the home. We've found lots of people wind up coming back to get something important. It's only human. You're certainly not the first person." He winked and waved the car back on the property.

They sent Meredith into the house and she returned with the purse from amidst three firefighters getting ready to tent the house. The firefighters waved at the family as Meredith got in the car and Donovan tapped the button to restart the engine and drive away. They pulled out and started the trip again. "We're going to drop you off, shima-sani Alice. Then eight hours from now, we'll be in California!" Donovan smiled back to the car through the rear view mirror. He politely winked at Alice, although unmoving in her chair. Donovan didn't mind. The rest of the car was also silent. Meredith was sending messages on her phone. The twins were engrossed in some game between them as they exchanged a slight shove in the back seat. Donovan and Amber opened the windows of the car to let in the air. This was a tradition between them. When they left before a burn, they opened the air to smell it, to get a sense of what the moment, what the atmosphere, was like before they had to start over. This year was different. They could smell the smoke from the fire that had already been started somewhere in the brush. Donovan coughed slightly, and Amber put her hand on his shoulder. They exchanged an exasperated and loving glance between them as they drove away from the flames. They would be back in a few weeks to start all over again, to replant and grow their lives again in one fashion or another, always the same and always different, like the many generations before them.

About the Authors

Jessica (Tyner) Mehta, born and raised in Oregon and a citizen of the Cherokee Nation, is a multi-award-winning interdisciplinary artist, author, and storyteller. She has received several writer-in-residencies around the world which were pivotal in supporting her writing of 15 published books. She is currently the post-graduate research representative at the Centre for Victorian Studies at the University of Exeter, England. She is the first Native American to serve in this role at the largest institutional Victorian research center in Great Britain. Her doctoral research addresses the intersection of eating disorders and poetry. Learn more about Jessica at her website, www.thischerokeerose.com, where you will find links to her books, upcoming projects, and the Emmy award winning documentary on her life and work from Osiyo Television.

Lydia K. Valentine is a writer, editor, educator, and dramaturg. Born and raised in Aliquippa, PA, and a proud Quip for life, she now makes her home in the beautifully rainy Pacific Northwest. Lydia is honored to have been selected as the 2021-2023 Tacoma Poet Laureate, a role that combines civic and community engagement with spreading love of poetry. More about Lydia, including information about her debut poetry collection, *Brief Black Candles*, can be found on her website: Lyderaryink.com and via socials @lyderaryink.

Kaia Valentine is a poet and short story author from Tacoma, Washington. She has a bachelor's degree in political science and philosophy, which culminated in a successful thesis on the modern phenomenon of transracialism. She values spirituality, intersectionality, emotional intelligence, anti-colonialism, and deep dissections of American culture. Her greatest joys in life are family, her wonderful pets, her superbly supportive girlfriend, Heather, literature, music, and the power that stems from trained critical thinking.

Claudine Griggs is the Writing Specialist at the Daniel Morgan Graduate School of National Security in D.C., and her publications include three nonfiction books about transsexuals along with a couple dozen articles on writing, teaching, and other topics. She also writes fiction and science fiction, her first-love genre as a teenager. Her novel *Don't Ask, Don't Tell* is available now. Her story "Helping Hand" was featured in Lightspeed Magazine and was made into a an animated short for the Netflix show Love, Death & Robots. Her story "Raptures of the Deep" was featured in Mountain Island Magazine. "Maiden Voyage of the Fearless" was featured in *Strongly Worded Women: The Best of The Year of Publishing Women: An Anthology*. Griggs earned her BA and MA in English at California State Polytechnic University, Pomona.

Ayodele Nzinga is an arts and culture theoretician/ practitioner working at the intersections of cultural production, community development, and community wellbeing to foster transformation in marginalized communities. Nzinga holds a Masters in Fine Arts in Writing and Consciousness and Doctorate of Philosophy in Transformative Education & Change; she resides in Oakland, CA. Described as a renaissance

woman, Ayodele is a producing director, playwright, poet, dramaturg, actress, performance consultant, arts educator, community advocate, and a culture bearing anchor.

TJ Berg is a molecular and cellular biologist working and writing in Sweden. She is a graduate of the Odyssey Writing Workshop. Her short fiction has appeared in *Talebones* (for which it received an honorable mention in *The Year's*

Best Fantasy and Horror), *Tales of the Unanticipated, Electric Velocipede, Daily Science Fiction, Caledonia Dreamin', Sensorama, Thirty Years of Rain, Tales to Terrify, New Myths,* and *Diabolical Plots.* When not writing or doing science, she can be found stravaigin the world, cooking, or hiking. She can be found on the web at www.infinity-press.com.

Zach Murphy is a Hawaii-born writer who somehow ended up in the chilly yet charming city of St. Paul, Minnesota. He has a background in film and prides himself on writing tales with a cinematic touch. He lives with his wonderful wife, Kelly, and they enjoy making friends with neighborhood cats. You can check out his film review blog, Fade to Zach.

Joanna Michal Hoyt lives with her family on a Catholic Worker farm in rural northern New York where she spends her days tending goats, gardens, and guests and her evenings reading and writing odd stories. Her short fiction has appeared in publications including *Mysterion*, *On Spec*, and *After Dinner Conversation*. Propertius

Press will publish her historical novel *Cracked Reflections* in May 2021. Read more at joannamichalhoyt.com

Simon J. Plant is a 20-something Aussie expat living in NYC with his husband and cat. By day he's a ballet dancer, performing in theaters around the world. By night he writes weird stuff and reads way too much Stephen King. Visit his author site to find out more at simonjplant.com

Huda Tariq is a professional woman all the way from Pakistan. She has a degree in biology (specifically botany) and works in education. She absolutely loves to write, all day, every day, irrespective of genres or platforms. She surrounds herself with infinite emotions. Though she's not a "Big Famous Writer," she believes she will be. Huda has been published in different magazines and journals. To have a peek at her pieces, you can follow her Instagram where she regularly posts her work: @huda.ht

Ndaba Sibanda is the author of *Notes, Themes, Things And Other Things, The Gushungo Way, Sleeping Rivers, Love O'clock, The Dead Must Be Sobbing, Football of Fools, Cutting-edge Cache, Of the Saliva and the Tongue, When Inspiration Sings In Silence, The Way Forward, The Ndaba Jamela Collections, Poetry Pharmacy,*

Sometimes Seasons Come With Unseasonal Harvests, As If They Minded, and *The Dangers Of Child Marriages: Billions Of Dollars Lost In Earnings And Human Capital.* Ndaba was nominated for the following awards: National Arts Merit Awards, The Pushcart Prize and Best of the Net. Sibanda's book *Notes, Themes, Things And Other Things: Confronting Controversies, Contradictions And Indoctrinations* was considered for The 2019 Restless Book Prize for New Immigrant Writing in Nonfiction. Ndaba's other forthcoming book, *Cabinet Meetings: Of Big And Small Preys*, was considered for The Graywolf Press Africa Prize 2018.

Sarah Jane Justice is a South Australian writer with an array of credits to her name. Starting out in performance arts, she lists three studio releases of original music to her name, as well as a science-fiction themed cabaret show that appeared in the 2016 Adelaide Fringe Festival. Although she continues to remain active as a performer, Sarah's focus has since turned to the written word. Her poetry and short fiction have been published in many journals, and she has recently discovered a fondness for speculative fiction, seeing her work featured in collections from Hawk and Cleaver, Black Hare Press, and Eerie River Publishing. In between performance commitments, and working on a full-length fiction project, Sarah has been managing production for 'Cracks in our Shadows', a mixed media exhibition created in collaboration with photographer Phillip Walker.

Fable Tethras is a journalist-turned-author who writes depressing science fiction and less depressing fantasy. Their short story, "Shrinking," was awarded an honorable mention in the L Ron Hubbard's Writers of the Future Contest. They live in Albuquerque, NM, where they spends most of their time writing or playing board games. Fable can be found on Twitter (@FableTethras) and Facebook.

Joann Renee Boswell is a natural light photographer and poet with over a dozen poems published and a book of poetry (with photography!), *Cosmic Pockets*. She served as one of the poetry editors for the Spring 2020 *VoiceCatcher* issue and started as poetry editor for *Untold Volumes* at Christian Feminism Today beginning June 2020. She enjoys rainy days filled with coffee, books, handholding, moody music, and sci-fi shows.

Eric Witchey has made a living as a freelance writer and communication consultant for over 25 years. In addition to producing many corporate non-fiction titles, he has sold more than 150 short stories and several novels. His stories have appeared in ten genres and on five continents. He has received recognition from New Century Writers, Writers of the Future, Writer's Digest, The Eric Hoffer Prose Award program, Short Story America, The Irish Aeon Awards, and other organizations. His How-To articles have appeared in *The Writer Magazine*, *Writer's Digest Magazine*, and other print and online magazines. When not teaching or writing, he spends his time fly fishing or restoring antique, model locomotives.

Janet Burroway is the author of plays, poetry, children's books, and eight novels including *The Buzzards*, *Raw Silk*, *Opening Nights*, *Cutting Stone* (all Notable Books of The New York Times Book Review), and most recently *Bridge of Sand*. Her plays have received readings and productions in Chicago, New York, London, San Francisco and Los Angeles. Her *Writing Fiction*, now in its ninth edition, is the most widely used creative writing text in America, and *Imaginative Writing* is in its fourth edition. She is author of the memoir *Losing Tim* (Think Piece Press, 2014). Winner of the 2014 Lifetime Achievement Award in Writing from the Florida Humanities Council, she is Robert O. Lawton Distinguished Professor Emerita at Florida State University.

Mike Jack Stoumbos is an emerging fiction author disguised as a believably normal high school teacher. He lives in western Washington with his wife and their parrot, and he can be found @MJStoumbos on Twitter and as Mike Jack Stoumbos (Author) on Facebook. He's the author of *The Baron Would Be Proud* (2012). Recently, he has been publishing short stories in anthologies and is seeking representation for new science fiction novels. Mike Jack continues to write and edit academic content for various groups, enjoys beta reading and workshopping new content, and coaches creative writing and RPG development for students when he gets the chance.

Koraly Dimitriadis is a poet, writer and actor and the author of the poetry books Just Give Me The Pills and Love and F--k Poems (which has also been translated into Greek). These poetic works form the basis of her theatre show "I say the wrong things all the time". She also makes films of her poems. She is a freelance opinion writer who has been published widely across the Australian media, with international publications in The Washington Post. She was the recipient of the UNESCO City of Literature residency (Krakow) in 2019 for her debut fiction manuscript, *Divided Island*. www.koralydimitriadis.com

Heather S. Ransom has served as a middle school science and careers teacher for twenty-seven years, allowing Heather an intimate look into the minds of thousands of young adults, most of whom are desperate to find their place in a society constantly changing around them. Many have found escape, ideas for facing challenges, or simply hope for a future where they can make a difference, through reading. So every year, even though she's teaching science, Heather has her classes read. And they imagine together what their futures might hold, telling stories about advances in technology that could change their world. Her novels *Going Green, Greener,* and *Back to Green* are available now.

Kate Maxwell is yet another teacher with writing aspirations. She's been published and awarded in Australian and International literary magazines such as The Chopping Blog, Hecate, Blood and Bourbon, fourW, and Social Alternatives. Kate's interests include film, wine, and sleeping. Her first poetry anthology, to be published with Interactive Publications,  Brisbane is forthcoming in 2021. She can be found at https://kateswritingplace.com/publications

Bethany Lee lives and writes in Oregon's beautiful Willamette Valley and draws inspiration from her work as a hospice harpist and choral accompanist and from a life filled with the practice of paying attention. Her poetry collection, *The Breath Between: An Invitation to Mystery and Joy*, was released from Fernwood Press in May 2019. Her latest work in progress is a memoir of the sabbatical year her family spent at sea. Keep an eye out for it and her forthcoming poetry collection, *Etude for Belonging: Poems for Courage and Hope*. She manages all this thanks to a consistently casual attitude toward housekeeping and her extraordinarily supportive partner, Bryan.

Benjamin Gorman is the author of the novels *The Sum of Our Gods*, *Corporate High School*, *The Digital Storm: A Science Fiction Reimagining of William Shakespeare's The Tempest*, *Don't Read This Book*, and the poetry collection *When She Leaves Me*. *Corporate High School* became an Amazon bestseller in 2016, and *The Digital Storm* was named a "Top Five Book Pick" by the San Diego Union Tribune. Benjamin is a high school English teacher. He lives in Independence, Oregon with his son, Noah. Benjamin believes in  human beings and the power of their stories. He places his confidence in his students and the world they will choose to create if given the chance.

Zack Dye is or has been an attorney, author/poet, bar owner, tax accountant, international business liaison, teacher, researcher, traveler, soccer coach and editor. He is a restless mind and soul who hopes to someday figure out what the hell he's doing on this planet. He has a bachelor's degree in economics and American studies from Tufts University, where he took a special interest in English literature and minority studies. Since then he has worked in Europe and South America before being admitted to the New York State Bar. He is close with his family and friends, trying to be a good son, uncle, dogfather and, in general, confidant to others who are equally confused about what this planet Earth is about.

Viveca Shearin started off as a freelance editor who joined Not a Pipe Publishing to work on a single novel and has worked her way to the top. In 2020 she was promoted to co-publisher and co-owner. She lives in Brooklyn, New York. When she's not working, Viveca can often be found with a big mug of tea (or coffee), her face buried in a good book or video game, and her beloved cat nearby for company. Follow her on twitter @ShearinViveca or on Facebook.

Our Next Anthology

We're so glad you've enjoyed our previous anthologies, *Strongly Worded Women*, *Shout*, and now *Denial Kills*. For our next anthology, we want to do something a bit more novel (see what we did there?). This time, the stories will be nested, one within the other, like Russian nesting dolls. So here's what you need to do: Write a story, 3k words or less, in which, at roughly the two-thirds mark, a character tells another character a story to illustrate a point. Only don't write that story-within-a-story. Someone else's story will be plugged in there! And someone else's will be plugged into theirs. And so on. Then, the last third of your story will continue when the character responds to/ignores/fails to understand the story-within-the-story which *you haven't even read*. And the end of *your* story will be the story another character responds to/ignores/fails to understand in someone else's story! Write in any genre; it's fine if a character in a sci-fi tells a fantasy story which includes a character who tells a Western which includes a character who tells a murder mystery which includes a character who tells a story that's historical fiction! You won't know which story will be set within yours and which story will envelope yours, so we hope this will be just as much fun for you as it will be for every other reader! It will be the ultimate celebration of storytelling. Send your story to @NotAPipePublishing with the subject line: Nesting Doll Anthology. (We'll choose a more fitting title for the anthology once we decide on the structure of the overarching narrative of all the stories.) Submissions will be accepted until August 1st, 2021.

As always, our authors retain the rights to their work, and anthology contributors receive equal shares of the royalties from sales.

A little tip for being included: Make sure your characters, the setting, and the plot in the first two thirds is memorable enough that a reader will recognize them even with a bunch of stories shoehorned into the middle of yours. Admit it! You're excited about this writing challenge, aren't you? And we bet you know another writer who you'd like to see included inside or outside of your story, so share this announcement with them, too.

Our anthologies have been packed with phenomenal, high-quality work, and the themes have been pretty heavy. We fought to make sure more women's voices were being read. We shouted against the rising tide of fascism. We screamed about the danger of denial. Now let's celebrate the way narratives are such an essential part of the human experience that our lives are stories within stories within stories within stories within stories...